WHEN GOD
CALLS
A Collection of
Life Changing Experiences
Led by God

WHEN GOD CALLS

A Collection of
Life Changing Experiences
Led by God

Dena Moscola
and the Contribution Team

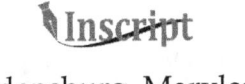

Inscript

Bladensburg, Maryland

When God Calls

Copyright 2023 by Resolutions Coaching & Training

All rights reserved

Hardcover ISBN 978-1-957497-18-1

Paperback ISBN 978-1-957497-32-7

Published in the United States of America

This book is humbly dedicated to
my daughter
Nicole,
my greatest gift from God!

Contents

Acknowledgments

With deep gratitude, I thank the Contribution Team for devoting their hearts, time, and energy to sharing their personal stories and making this book possible.

Shannon Baum

James Martinez

Ralph Martinez

Diana Baum

Tina

Larry Socea

Roberta Carter

Donna Nelson Castelonia

Glenn Crooker

Liza Davis

Phillip and Dianna

Thank you also to the Scripture Team, who joined me in diving deeper into some of the stories to match them to Biblical Scriptures: Roberta Carver, Shannon Baum, and Diana Baum.

And sending lots of love to those who shared Godly guidance, strong faith, role modeling, and friendship that has had a significant impact on my faith: Laurel Devine, Janine Schindler, Angela Kubiski, Shannon Baum, Heather Clark-Peckerman, Laura Lutz and Maurissa Maestas.

Part 1:

Introduction

By Dena Moscola

Born and raised in NJ, this full-blooded Italian was raised Catholic, sort of. Being Catholic to my family seemed to mean we had to believe in God, go to Sunday School and Church, receive our sacraments, and don't use the "F" word! That's it! I don't remember talking much about God in our home. Occasionally, my mother would say to my brother or me, "God is watching you," or "God will punish you!" But those words held little weight. My belief in God was blurry then, but the belief stayed with me. I do remember my mother taught me to pray when I needed help or when family members needed healing. I thought that was enough.

This level of faith stayed with me as I grew up. I prayed directly to God. I believed Jesus died on the cross but didn't understand what to do with that. I never considered Jesus while I prayed. Admittingly, I thought I was cutting out the middleman! Thankfully, I've learned a lot since, but then, I didn't know what I didn't know.

I knew God was my protector. This grew over the years, and that is not because of church or Bible studies. I stopped going to church after I received Confirmation and didn't start reading the Bible for many years. But I knew God was real and with me.

Over the years, I began to recognize life-changing guidance from God. The more I recognized it, the more it happened. Then my curiosity started increasing, so I did (and still do) my best to learn as much as I could about God's intentions and law. My faith grew naturally and became unshakable. Now, my relationship with God is an incredible journey that keeps getting better and better.

As years went on, following God's guidance daily became a way of life for me. Following God's Commandments is part of it, but I'm also referring to guidance on decisions big and small.

One day, my friend Laurel said something profound to me that left me confused until years later. We had been close friends for over ten years and also worked together a few times. She had (and still has) my utmost respect because she is a woman of unwavering faith with a strong sense of self. She is highly confident, financially wise, happily married for decades, and an amazing mom who enjoys a close relationship with her two children. I'll never forget her words: "... It's not about me. I know nothing. It is all because of God. God tells me what I'm supposed to do, and I listen. Every day I get up and ask God what he wants me to do. God guides me. God gets the credit for everything!"

I was so surprised at her statement that I said nothing.

Ever. But it stayed with me, and I wondered about it. I thought, how could a woman so strong, happy, and successful have so little confidence in herself? Why is she not realizing how amazing she is? Why is she not taking credit for anything? I admired her faith yet didn't understand it as well as I thought I did, so I also didn't understand her statement. But, since I knew her so well, I couldn't accept that her words came from a lack of confidence. Looking back, I realize I was the one lacking confidence for not asking her then to explain her comment to me. But the more I thought about it, the more I realized how strong her faith was and that God CAN and SHOULD be a part of our daily lives. I wanted that level of faith that Laurel had.

But that wasn't easy for me, then. I grew up being told I could do anything I set my mind to and, therefore, had many accomplishments. I was used to receiving tremendous praise personally and professionally and, in turn, made it a point to praise others generously. But Laurel's comments weighed heavy on my heart. As time went on, it led me to reflect on unusual occurrences that happened in my life — odd, "gut" feelings that I followed that changed my life for the best. But when I gave it serious consideration, I realized my stomach played no part in that! Some people said to me, "the Universe is guiding you." I bought that for a while. Seemed like a simple, noncontroversial thought. Then it all connected; the Universe is air! God created the Universe;

GOD is guiding me and HAS BEEN all my life!

Inside, I felt like the lightbulb went on, and I finally understood Laurel's profound comment. My faith jumped up a thousand notches and began growing at lightning speeds! This was a feeling of immense exhilaration! Now, I know nothing is too small for God. God goes before us and has our paths planned out perfectly. Why would anyone not want to follow Him?

Trust in the Lord with all thine heart; and lean not unto thine own understanding. In all thy ways acknowledge Him, and He shall direct thy paths (Proverbs 3: 5-6 KJV)

I began planning less and being more open to God's callings and guidance regularly. I began seeking it through prayer, journaling, meditation, and just plain awareness. Things fell into place faster. And when challenges erupted, I learned not to worry, not to hold on too tight. I learned to release control. I learned to trust God more and more.

As a result, stress diminished, worry vanished, and trust took over! Soon, following God became a lifestyle for me, and when I finally picked up a Bible and started going to church (late bloomer!), I learned why and how it was all happening. It was like putting pieces of the puzzle together.

That story is a bit backward compared to others, but how and when we get to God really doesn't matter. As long as we find and embrace Him. Everyone has their own story, and all stories are the right stories.

Fast forward to this book. This book idea came to me in dreams three nights in a row, where I believe God planted the idea for me and then gave me the details. The first dream was telling me I would write a book. This woke me up in the middle of the night and made me laugh to myself because I had no desire to write a book, so I dismissed the idea. Instantly, the idea grew stronger inside of me. Within moments, I realized, "Wait, this must be coming from God." And I suddenly felt open to the idea of writing a book but had no idea what to write about! I let it go and thought that if it was God calling, then God would provide the topic and the guidance.

The next night, I dreamt about the topic. This wasn't the most comfortable for me because I was used to writing books on leadership, which are much more tangible and widely accepted in the work world. God's callings in my life is a topic that is personal to me, and talking about them would expose so much of my deepest beliefs. Then I realized how important it would be if others learned to trust and follow God's guidance more. I thought maybe a book like that could inspire others. I felt a passion growing inside me. God was asking me to write about the power that fueled my world, His power, that I habitually kept quiet about but started realizing I shouldn't! What an honor!

I agreed to write the book. But I had no idea what to do

next. On the 3rd night, God revealed the entire outline of this book in my dream. I woke up knowing it was time to move forward with helping others recognize when God is guiding, calling, talking, showing—whatever you want to call it! My excitement grows continuously, hoping that this book clarifies how to recognize God more, grow closer to God, and feel more comfortable acknowledging God's presence, participation, and gifts! God is good. God loves you. God has a plan for you. That plan is there for you to accept if you want.

First, in this book, you will find answers to common questions about receiving God's guidance, such as:

- What is a calling like?
- Why would God guide me?
- How do I refocus back on God?
- Is it really God?
- How do I be more receptive?

Then, I will share a few of the many callings from God that transformed my life to be more wonderful than I hoped. And to show how God calls us all differently, you will read stories from others that follow God's callings. Learn about their unique experiences, challenges, and the incredible results that followed. You'll notice each calling is so very different. Each required varying levels of change, effort, and trust. You'll see a variety of emotions experienced, including fear, confusion, shame, excitement, gratitude, and more. Some of the callings demanded tremendous inner work. Others required risk. Some folks share how God guided them daily, while others share their call to follow God as a lifestyle. All stories involve acting on faith, and all results transformed lives. All stories are written in truth as perceived by the contributing author. Scriptures have been added to connect you to specific parts of the Bible that reinforce the message.

Whether you are a beginner Christian, have had a relationship with God all your life, are somewhere in between, or are just simply curious, we hope this book helps you deepen your connection to God, which can always be stronger!

Chapter 1

Unanswered Questions

By Dena Moscola

- What is a calling like?
- Why Would God Guide Me?
- 4 Ways to Refocus Back to God
- Bottom Line: Is It God or Not?
- Exercise: Increase Your Receptiveness to God

What is a Calling Like?

Before we dive into more experiences, let's start off by addressing some questions bound to be circling in the minds of many.

So, what is all this talk about "a calling"? Did you ever get an idea that felt more like an instruction than a thought? Or maybe it was so unexpected it surprised you? Or it was puzzling because it was so completely opposite of what you were thinking? Or maybe it scared you because it felt right, but you were afraid of failing, and you thought about all the reasons it wouldn't work, yet it persisted and maybe got a little louder? Or was it so quiet that it was almost hard to hear? And when you tried to hear it again, it was just a distant memory. Maybe its effect lingered. Maybe it disappeared. Just maybe it was so far away from the path you were already on that it seemed impossible to accomplish, and you thought, "I could never do that!"

If you answered yes to any of these scenarios or thought of your own scenario, I ask you, where did this come from? You may rationalize that it came from you, but did it? Your ego may want to take all the credit. That's a natural and common reaction, but is it accurate? God talks to all of us. He is guiding us and laying out His path for us. But it is up to us to follow. Sometimes it is easy. Sometimes it is confusing or the opposite of what we had in mind. But it is always in our best interest and for the greater good.

God is always with us, and He guides us along His path. But often, His guidance is hard to hear or recognize, so it can easily get overlooked. With a few simple tips and practice, God's word can become more and more clear to each of us.

God's path isn't always what we imagine, which can cause uncertainty. This can be scary and confusing, leading one to avoid the guidance that God so graciously provides for us. Or we can become stubborn because we feel the need to stick to our plan. These doubting thoughts make it easier to keep doing what we've been doing instead of following the calling. But when you follow God's calling with trust, true trust, God will light the path for you. But it starts with trust. Trust that God has the path paved for you, even if you do not know what that looks like at first. Trust that our Lord Jesus Christ has gone before us and knows what's ahead, and it's going to be alright — or amazing!

And the Lord, he it is that doth go before thee; he will be with thee, he will not fail thee, neither forsake thee: fear not, neither be dismayed (Deuteronomy 31:8).

I will go before thee, and make the crooked places straight: I will break in pieces the gates of brass, and cut in sunder the bars of iron (Isaiah 45:2).

When you take the first step, which is to agree to follow God's calling, God's light will shine and get brighter and brighter for you to see clearer and clearer. This light will reveal itself differently for each of us. Remember, God's path for you is customized, so you will need to discern what is God and what is not. The one thing we can always be certain of is that God will NEVER steer you from his commandments. God will only steer you towards good. Any other direction, even if it feels good to you, is not God. Remember, just because it feels good doesn't mean it is. The adversary will always tempt us, but we need to see past that and know that God's way, no matter how unusual, difficult, or long that may be, will always serve us best in the end.

Trust in the Lord with all your heart, and lean not on your own understanding: In all your ways acknowledge Him and He shall direct your paths. Do not be wise in your own eyes. (Proverbs 3:5-7 NKJV)

Here are some examples of how God's light may reveal itself:

- A persistently repetitive thought, theme, or message that tugs on your heart or in your mind and gets stronger and stronger.
- Friends may be continuously giving you a message.
- Strangers may randomly show up to help you with a task, idea, advice, or goal.
- Unexpected ideas may pop into your brain, perhaps at odd times, like while you are sleeping, driving, in the shower, etc.
- Dreams may reveal a vision, next steps, and/or guidance.
- Unexpected opportunities to get you to the next steps.
- Surprise situations one might say are "coincidences" but are reassuring.
- Current circumstances that are not helping may go away quietly or abruptly, whether you like it or not.

- Feelings of discomfort, tension, or even anxiety may stir inside of you.
- A good feeling of peace or comfort may be present, letting you know you are on track.

This list can go on and on. The bottom line is that everyone is different, and only you know how God's guidance comes through for you and when. And can you be 100% sure? Some say yes, absolutely. Some are not sure. The key is to pay attention to what is happening around you and within you to be sure to catch God's messages. The secular world is quite good at distracting our attention away from God. This happens through social media, television, music, peer pressure, your own critical thoughts, etc. We must not give in to distractions. But if you fall into temptation (as all of us humans do!), you must return to God's calling as soon as you realize you have strayed.

Why Would God Guide Me?

Did you ever think, "But why would God pick me to guide?" And how do you know it is really God guiding you? Could it be your imagination? Did you ever think, "God is busy with other bigger, more important things than me"?

It's easy to rule out God by thinking things like "It's all in my mind" or "if I admit to hearing a voice, I am crazy!", "I don't deserve something as good as this," or "I have no idea how to do this," "I'll never be able to do this," "I'm not good enough for this," or "why would God talk to me?" Or... or... or... or...!

Those are quite common thoughts to have, BUT they are wrong! When God provides a blessing to you, such as guidance, a calling, a plan, a gift, etc., it will be good! Real good! AND the devil will try to counter this goodness by distracting you or giving you thoughts of inadequacy, shame, or doubt. The devil's desire is to turn you away from God through distraction, temptation, confusion, and feelings of unworthiness.

Perhaps you have done some things that you know God would disapprove of. Or maybe you have a lifestyle you know is against God's wishes, and you do not want to give that lifestyle up. Perhaps you feel shame or guilt. Or maybe you just feel you are not worth God's time and attention. Believe it or not, those are common thoughts that can cause anyone to ignore God's guidance and avoid giving Him credit for the miracles you witness and experience. You attribute them to coincidences instead or ignore them completely. The good news is that you are wrong!! God loves you. Yes, YOU! God loves us all. We are God's children. He sees our iniquities, which we all have, and he deeply loves us anyway! He also sees your potential and wants you to fulfill it. He has made us all capable of anything he places on our hearts. He will never give you a dream that you cannot achieve. You may need to learn a few things. You may even stumble and fall a few times before getting there, but that's ok. That does not mean failure. That means there is more to learn.

Trust that God is here for you. Believe in Him. Trust Him. If you do, He will show up for you in ways you never imagined. You will have the guidance you need. The right people and opportunities will appear. You are worthy. No matter what you see in yourself, God sees you better. Much better.

"For God so loved the world, that he gave his only begotten Son, that whosoever believeth in him should not perish, but have everlasting life" (John 3:16).

Repent of your wrongdoings, and you will be forgiven by God. Yes, anything! Then it is important for you to walk away from your past. Let go of the guilt and shame. Holding on to it will prevent God's greatness from shining through for you. Your past ends with repenting and is forgiven, and you are then free to move forward. He will change your heart and bring you peace. Know that God will light the path for you.

God wants to help you and guide you. He wants to protect you and see you happy. God is good, even to you. You are worthy of God's love not because of what you have or have not done, but because that is the kind of God He is.

For thou, Lord, art good, and ready to forgive; and plenteous in mercy unto all them that call upon thee (Psalms 86: 5).

But thou, O Lord, art a God full of compassion, and gracious, long suffering, and plenteous in mercy and truth (Psalms 86:15).

God is your creator. He sent us Jesus, His only son, to live as we live and feel what we feel, including the temptations to do wrong. Jesus died for our sins through his own blood on the cross. That was a sacrifice that takes away our sins, even yours, once you believe that and repent and seek God's path.

You must hold focus and not give in to such critical thinking. Prepare yourself because these temptations will happen. It will be up to you to keep your eye on God the entire time. And remember, when you catch yourself in doubt or off focus, simply refocus. Perfection is not the mission. Refocusing is.

Simply refocus. Ha! Easier said than done, right?

So how do you refocus? There are four keys to help refocus back on God. All four keys work separately and together. Together is best, but we are all human and sometimes it takes a while to build new habits.

Here they are:

4 Keys to Refocus Back to God

1. Ask for it
2. Be Around the Right People
3. Live the Right Lifestyle
4. Think the Right Thoughts

1: Ask for It! The BEST way is to simply ask God to help you get back to His blessing and help you ignore the distractions. You can formally pray for strength to avoid distractions and stay on His path for you. You can also just ask as if you were talking to your friend. Because, after all, you ARE talking to your friend! Remember, it's God's message specifically designed for you. He wants you to succeed, so He will help you stay on track if you ask for that help. And you will succeed if you follow because God has already gone ahead of you and paved your path. Stay close to God in prayer or conversation, even while you are focused. This will minimize or eliminate temptation.

2. Be Around the Right People: Besides asking God to help you refocus, it is important to surround yourself with others who live for God's truth, so they can remind you to get back to focus. These reminders will come through you asking for them, which is welcome since we believers understand constant, daily temptations. Reminders will also happen organically just by being in the presence of other believers. Reminders will also show up for you because believers often lead by example. You will watch them deal with the challenges of their lives and learn how to get through with God on your side.

Believers share a bond that is highly supportive during times of doubt, feeling lost, worrying, and crisis. Believers will help each other shift their thoughts back to God. This will reduce or eliminate dwelling in tough times. Dwelling on perceived problems causes spiraling, which leads to more worry, fear, and wrong choices. Dwelling is a distraction that will take you off the path. Dwelling can lead to depression.

You will always move towards what you focus on most, so doesn't it make sense to surround yourself with Godly people who will naturally serve as a reminder to focus on God? Believers remind each other to focus on God and pray for each other.

Surrounding yourself with the right people does not necessarily mean eliminating loved ones that think differently than you. It may. But maybe not. It is not uncommon to have family members and friends who are not focused on God. That is their free will. You must discern who to spend the most time with and how to spend time with them. Are they tempting you into thinking or acting in ways that are not aligned with God's way? If so, this is something to seriously consider. Being tempted in the wrong direction may unconsciously lead you down the wrong path. It will make it harder to receive God's calling and may even cause you to miss it completely.

Additionally, temptation is contagious, whether in the form of thinking or actions. At first, it may be easy to stand your ground, but as time goes on, that discipline can slowly decrease without you even realizing it. Then suddenly, you find yourself slipping. Other times, it happens fast, and you have difficulty wondering how it happened.

Either way, after a while, you may look back with regret and have a more difficult time finding your way back if you're not lost completely. Conformity is human nature, and you may not realize it is happening, despite your strength and best intentions.

Is it worth the risk? You will need to decide if spending time with this type of person or group of people is best for you. Are boundaries needed, and if so, what type of boundaries are best?

...bad company corrupts good character (1 Corinthians 15:33 NIV)

Make no friendship with an angry man: And with a furious man thou shalt not go: Lest thou learn his ways, And get a snare to thy soul. Be not thou one of them that strikes hands, or of them that are sureties for debts. (Proverbs 22: 24–26)

Still, some nonbelievers do not pose any negative temptation. They, too, have a lifestyle of striving to do the right thing and are a pleasure to be around. You will probably inspire each other. No harm done. As a bonus, you may even serve as a godly example to them, leading them to learn more about God.

When we talk about surrounding ourselves with the right people, let's highlight one important fact: no one is perfect! Believer or nonbeliever—we all make mistakes and sin. We are human! The key difference is that a true committed believer in Jesus, our Savior, will always seek to please God, return to God, and be open to the support that brings them back to God. Fellow believers often inspire each other toward God's way and provide the comfort of like-minded thinking. This leads to an easier time hearing, seeing, or feeling God's blessings and guidance. It basically helps build and maintain godly habits.

Remember, we become who we are surrounded by. Choose wisely!

He that walketh with wise men shall be wise: but a companion of fools shall be destroyed. (Proverbs 13:20)

3. Live the Right Lifestyle: Strive to live a lifestyle that supports God's truth. As important as it is to surround yourself with the right people, it is necessary to live the right lifestyle. Both can go hand in hand and be practiced separately as well.

In this the children of God are manifest, and the children of the devil: whosoever doeth not righteousness is not of God, neither he that loveth not his brother (1 John 3:10).

Are your actions and habits aligned with God's Laws? You may have a few things that need some adjustments. We all do. That is ok; we are not perfect. Being aware of where change is needed is critical, and working towards improvement brings lifestyle decisions that please God. Maybe you want to adjust one thing at a time, or maybe you want to dive in and clean the slate to start fresh. That is up to you, but the more you live up to God's wishes, the easier and more frequently God's messages will be evident. Surrounding yourself with the right people will often make this goal easier.

For not the hearers of the law are just before God, but the doers of the law shall be justified (Romans 2:13).

Another critical piece to living the right lifestyle is giving back. Are you contributing to those less fortunate than you? If not, find ways to help others feel better or do better. You can contribute through service, kindness, and finances. The options are endless. The key is serving a cause (or 2!) bigger than you. Taking the focus off yourself helps to open your heart to more grace. This pleases God.

Living a lifestyle that pleases God will ultimately fill your soul with deeper peace. In this peace, God's grace and guidance can be easier to recognize.

Are you tithing to your Church? Tithing shows God that you realize everything you receive comes from him, and you appreciate that by giving some of it back.

And all the tithe of the land, whether of the seed of the land, or of the fruit of the tree, is the Lord's: it is holy unto the Lord (Leviticus 27:30).

Honour the Lord with thy substance, and with the first fruits of all thine increase: So shall thy barns be filled with plenty, and thy presses shall burst out with new wine (Proverbs 3: 9 -10).

4. Think the Right Thoughts: What we think creates our feelings, and our feelings lead to our actions. Remembering to communicate with our Lord, choosing the right people to surround ourselves with, and living the right lifestyle starts with our thoughts. We need to control our thinking. It is easy to fall victim to unrighteous thinking and lose control. It is easy to blame your behavior on your feelings. But it always comes back to your thoughts.

Thoughts = Feelings = Actions

The adversary will always be waiting in our minds for an opportunity to criticize, tempt, and confuse. And it can be overwhelming. You must fight that urge to listen to it. Take control and create your own thoughts. Ask God to take those destructive thoughts away and give you peace so you can get back on track.

I mentioned repenting earlier — turning over guilt, shame, and wrongdoings to God. That helps release a tremendous amount of critical destructive self-talk. When you surrender to God, he forgives you; you must remember to forgive yourself, also!

Other thought patterns that will block your callings are negative judgments towards others. It is so easy to judge another. You may think someone is ugly, good-looking, skinny, fat, short, tall, mean, rich, poor, stupid, talkative, quiet, bossy, selfish, irresponsible, etc. Perhaps you judge someone struggling with addiction, homelessness, or mental illness. Or you judge because of one's political beliefs, skin color, culture, gender, etc. The fact is, no one is perfect. The next fact is that people will think differently than you, look different, and act differently. We are not here to judge others. That is God's job, not ours. And remember — God doesn't see those differences in people. To him, we are all His children, either believers or not. The rest is insignificant.

That doesn't mean you need to agree with everyone. It means you need to release the judgment. You have the right to choose who you associate with. Those whom you choose to avoid do not need to be judged. You have the right to like some and not others. But you can still strive to love all. They are human, just like you. Whether they make mistakes or are just different than you, everyone is doing their best with the resources available to them. And that applies to everyone, even those who do wrong. That doesn't make it ok, but it releases judgment. Love thy neighbor. Pray for them.

Just as critical thoughts directed at yourself are destructive, so are critical thoughts toward others. How many times each day do you judge others? It can happen so quickly. For many, it's a go-to thought pattern or habit. Destructive.

It is not your place to judge others. That is God's job, and he will do it, no doubt. Releasing judgment isn't about ignoring wrongdoings. It is about releasing negative emotions towards others when they do not meet your expectations or standards. Remember that everyone is doing the best they can. To release judgment, try shifting your thoughts to curiosity, which often leads to understanding. Agreeing is not always possible, but judging is completely in your control. Ask God to help you by giving you the peace to let go of judgment and strength and courage to be curious and understanding instead. God will grant us the grace we need when we remember to ask for it.

But why dost thou judge thy brother? or why dost thou set at nought thy brother? for we shall all stand before the judgment seat of Christ" (Romans 14:10).

Judge not, that you be not judged. For with the judgment you pronounce you will be judged, and with the measure you use it will be measured to you. Why do you see the speck that is in your brother's eye, but do not notice the log that is in your own eye? Or how can you say to your brother, 'Let me take the speck out of your eye,' when there is the log in your own eye? You hypocrite, first take the log out of your own eye, and then you will see clearly to take the speck out of your brother's eye. (Romans 14:10)

If you find yourself judging others, try to take on another perspective. Ask yourself, how would Jesus view them or this situation? He would not judge. He would be curious and forgiving. The more kindness in your heart, the more likely you will please God and hear his guidance.

As you release judgment, resentment starts to naturally fade away. Resentment is a wasted emotion. It never serves or revenges the one you resent. It only keeps you in chains. Release judgment, and resentment melts away. And avoid revenge always.

Thinking of others in a Godlier way is not always easy, especially in a society that spotlights differences and wrong doings. Remember, God does not judge by skin color, race, gender, etc. We should not either. Asking God for patience and strength to avoid judgment is the best, most rewarding way to change your thinking. And a magical piece to this is that once you release judgment, your relationship with that person and/or others will organically improve. God works mysteriously wonderfully like that!!

Thou shalt love thy neighbor as thyself. There is none other commandment greater than these (Mark 12:31).

Bottom Line: Is it God or Not?

The best way to decipher God's messages against other possibilities is by how you feel. Consider how you feel about it when you have an idea or a dream or a heartfelt idea. Ignore it being unexpected, impossible, scary, or against the original plan. Ignore, for the moment, that you may not know how to make this happen or not have the skills/experience to accomplish this. Just think about the idea. Imagine accomplishing it. How does that make you feel? If you feel peace and goodness in your heart, and it is best for the greater good, chances are, it is God's doing!

I believe it is God when I think about the message, and my heart feels light and free, and the fear of not following becomes stronger than the fear of following. And most importantly, the request is aligned with God's Law.

Only you can discern God's presence in your life, but if you follow the recommendations in this book, chances are you will recognize God's calling faster and easier.

It's important to remember that God's calling may seem

impossible or may not make much logical sense. But that is ok. Those things will be taken care of and revealed as you go. Once you agree to your instructions with trust, God will light your way! Remember, with God, anything is possible!

Later, when the task or mission is accomplished, you will look back in amazement at how God showered you with blessings and changed you into becoming the perfect person to accomplish the task! And don't be surprised if He changed you along the way to becoming someone better than you imagined.

Exercise: Increasing Your Receptiveness to God's Callings

But if you have never heard God speak to you or felt His guidance, you are not alone. That doesn't mean God is not speaking to you. Being open to hearing God is necessary. Many say, "I pray all the time, but God never responds." Everyone is different, but God loves all his children and wants to guide you through the path he has chosen for you. Being open to talking WITH God more and not just to him may help you notice a difference.

One way to do this is to create a space daily where you can sit quietly with God. Make sure you are alone and free from distractions and interruptions. Silencing your phone will help. Many people find it best to do this first thing in the morning or at the end of the day. But anytime works.

Start off with a minute to two. This may seem uncomfortable. That's ok. You will get used to it and feel more comfortable. Feeling uncomfortable means you are becoming more open. Push through it. Gradually add a minute or two or more to each sitting. During this time, you can pray, or you can just sit quietly. Generally, this is called meditating with God.

When I first started this activity, I would simply ask, "Dear God, what messages do you have for me today?" As time went on, I learned this practice again and again from friends and Bible studies. Each time helped me get more comfortable with the process. I added prayers of gratitude and prayers to help others. The key is to get used to sitting quietly with God. Once, a church I attended offered one night per week where we could all come in with our blankets or mats and practice this exercise where we were just open to God's messages. Afterward, some would share their experience. Others just enjoyed the peace. It was a wonderful event.

Some other examples of wording you can use are below, but feel free to change it up to make it most comfortable for you:

- Dear Lord Jesus, please help me hear your voice and follow your ways.
- Heavenly Father, what is your plan for me today?

- Dear God, please clear the clutter in my mind and fill my heart with your wishes.
- God our Father, please remove the distractions in my life and help me see clearly so I can know what you want for me and from me and please give me the strength to follow you.
- My Dear Father, as I sit in silence, I question this exercise. Please help me have patience as you prepare me to increase my knowledge of your wishes for me.
- Dear Lord, help me have the strength to trust you and the memory to seek guidance from you

You might want to keep a journal nearby so you can make notes of any ideas or instructions that come to mind.

Chapter 2

A Lifetime of Callings

By Dena Moscola

- God Hijacked My Career Path
- A Visit from Jesus
- Getting Positioned for the Next Mission

God Hijacked My Career Path

During high school, my dream was to help people do their best in life and at work. As I was preparing to go away to college to make this dream come true, it slowly became evident that God wanted me to take a different path. I didn't realize it was God, but I kept getting a strong sensation to do things differently. I heard a voice in my mind saying, "Don't go away to college; your best education will be on the road." I thought I had imagined it since it made no sense and didn't match my plan. But it became a strong feeling inside of me, and I realized there was a higher calling. I didn't realize what that even meant, but despite the norms of society and my parents' expectations, I trusted it. Why? Because it felt right. It made little sense, and it was difficult to go in the opposite direction of my plan. But the inspiration was stronger than other people's opinions, and I knew if it didn't work out, college would still be an option. So, there was no harm in following it.

And I will bring the blind by a way that they knew not; I will lead them in paths that they have not known: I will make darkness light before them, and crooked things straight. These things will I do unto them, and not forsake them (Isaiah 42:16).

Having nothing to lose, I attended a local college, landed a job in human services, and got some valuable work experience, forgetting all about that previous "calling" to learn on the road. Strangely, I ended up on a road trip, but it wasn't my first choice. I was supposed to visit my friend in Colorado, but she had to cancel suddenly. My other friend in California was looking for someone to go on a road trip with that very same week. So off I went, on the road, exploring California. I'll never forget; the moment I crossed the Bay Bridge in San Francisco, I knew living there was my next step. A few months later, I landed a job there and moved to the Bay Area, having no idea that the "on-the-road education" was about to begin.

Howbeit when he, the Spirit of truth, is come, he will guide you into all truth: for he shall not speak of himself; but whatsoever he shall hear, that shall he speak: and he will shew you things to come (John

16:13).

Once there, I unexpectedly became heavily involved in a series of training in California and throughout the US on topics that were then unavailable in college curricula but completely aligned with the professional direction of my dreams. This was intense and lasted for several years. The topics provided multiple specialized certifications in employee and personal development. I acquired work around these topics and eventually had enough training, work, and life experience to launch my business in 1997. The business (Resolutions Coaching and Training) still exists today and focuses on leadership development and helping people be their best at work and in their personal life.

The steps of a good man are ordered by the LORD: And he delighteth in his way (Psalm 37:23).

The training I received on the road during those years was priceless because I had the privilege of training with the country's best practitioners in each modality. That business enabled me at a young age to make my own schedule, lead a stress-free life, and, most importantly, raise my daughter on my terms and not my employers!

Thinking back, all that started with an unexpected calling, "Your best education will be on the road." I blindly followed that calling, even though it made little sense then. It was risky, and others thought I was nuts! Years later, I realized God planted that guidance in my heart and guided me through that unusual educational tour that led to a fulfilling lifetime business of helping hundreds of thousands excel in their careers and life. Thank you, God!

"Trust in the Lord with all thine heart; and lean not unto thine own understanding. In all thy ways acknowledge him, And he shall direct thy paths" **(Proverbs 3:5-6).**

A Visit from Jesus

One late night in 2014, while I was sitting in bed, light on, unable to sleep, there was an unexpected flash. In a vision, I saw a man kneeling at the foot of the other side of my bed. He was in a white robe and had his hands folded. He said, "Trust me, please, please trust me. Please trust me." I had never had a vision before, but I felt comfortable with the experience for some reason. I knew it was Jesus, and at that moment, a calm, peaceful feeling overcame me. I found myself nodding slowly, saying, "OK." That's it. Just "OK." And then he was gone. I was completely unaware of how profound this experience was and how it would change my life. I didn't even think to tell anyone about it then. I just knew in my heart that from that point forward, I would trust Jesus, even though I didn't know what that meant!

For we are his workmanship, created in Christ Jesus

unto good works, which God hath before ordained that we should walk in them (Ephesians 2:10).

Getting Positioned for the Next Mission

A few months later, while vacationing with my daughter, I felt the calling again–"It's time to move." My life was full and happy at the time, but despite that, I followed the call. But to where? I started exploring options. Each idea excited me, but every effort towards learning about new places brought feelings of tension in my abdomen. It was very uncomfortable, almost painful, and made my research difficult to sit through. Accompanying this feeling were always the words "New Mexico" repeating in the back of my mind. I resisted because I did not want to move to New Mexico. Despite its magnificent views, my one brief visit there left me feeling like it was too mellow for my lifestyle. I didn't realize at the time that God was guiding me towards just that: a new, more relaxed lifestyle.

This tension and the message to move to New Mexico persisted. So, I surrendered to this idea of moving to New Mexico and instantly felt an inner peace deeper than I ever experienced! In less than 24 hours after deciding to move there, unexpected business opportunities popped up, enabling me to keep my clients and work virtually. Then I was offered a beautiful home in Northern New Mexico. Some thought I was crazy, others thought I was brave, but those who knew me knew I just had to follow this. Deep inside, I felt more scared to ignore it than to follow. Over the years, I have learned **when God calls, you go!**

> **"And when he putteth forth his own sheep, he goeth before them, and the sheep follow him: for they know his voice. And a stranger will they not follow, but will flee from him: for they know not the voice of strangers." (John 10:4-5)**

Four months later, I sold everything and moved to NM. My safety net plan was to go only for the summer, but after being there a nano second, I knew I was staying!

To this day, many people compliment my bravery for listening to the calling. My response is always the same: "It's not courage; it's fear — fear of ignoring the calling!"

Why fear? Because I had so many life-altering callings in my life that it literally scared me to risk missing the greatness that I knew would follow. I knew following kept me on God's path. Ignoring could lead me off God's path. That scared me. When God calls, He has a plan, He knows best, and God is ALWAYS good!! Like I said, **"when God calls, you go!"**

It didn't take long to see that God wanted me in New Mexico for some reason. I was blessed with the gift of paradise, and I had no idea why. From the moment I arrived in New Mexico, I was blown away by the magic of this incredibly scenic state, the comfort of dry, high-altitude living year-round, and the peace that comes from a laid-back culture. God was right; this lifestyle change was perfect for me, and so was the timing. I didn't realize it at the time, but He did! To this day, I give thanks to God daily (or more) and am filled with amazement! God is incredible. I often think, "Had I ignored God's calling, which made no sense at the time, I would never have received this incredible new life! Who knew?? (God knew!!!)

I will instruct thee and teach thee in the way which thou shalt go: I will guide thee with mine eye. (Psalm 32:8)

My move to New Mexico was approximately one year after I had the vision of Jesus asking me to trust him. After I moved, a dear friend sent me two gifts: a book titled "Jesus Calling" and a Bible. These gifts seemed daunting at the time but reminded me of Jesus asking me to trust him. So, I read these books, and my life started changing! Not only was I living in paradise, but at fifty years old, I was getting to know Jesus for the first time. The myths, puzzles, and assumptions that swirled in my head went away, and my trust and understanding grew deeper. The presence of Jesus in my life was growing, and my heart was overflowing with gratitude and amazement. Those who knew me then knew this was big, since my heart was already full of gratitude. But it kept getting better. My world (inside and out) was shifting drastically and overcoming me.

Simultaneously, my first friend in NM turned out to have a huge addiction to heroin and meth and came to me to help him through withdrawals. Others told me to walk away, but I felt that if God sent him to me, it was my place to do my best. But it was very frustrating because once I was able to encourage him to commit to rehab, getting him there was a new set of frustrations because of many holes in the system. This bothered me so much that I created a plan to start an agency to fill the gaps and provide faster help to those looking to go into recovery. Unfortunately, I had to put that plan to rest because it was too big to tackle as a newbie to the state.

A few years later, after I was more acclimated to the NM culture and dynamics, an unexpected opportunity literally fell in my lap. A brand-new non-profit, Espanola Pathways Shelter (EPS), was looking for an Executive Director to open a homeless shelter in a Northern New Mexican city in dire need. This grabbed my attention and my heart. God was calling again. But, there was doubt... I completely forgot about the plan I had put together four years prior. Instead, all I kept thinking was, "A homeless shelter? Not on my bucket list!" But I knew the needs of this city. Espanola: The Heroin Capital of the United States, riddled with genera-tional poverty and addiction, and it never had a homeless shelter. This was my chance to contribute, which might be why God called me to New Mexico???

To my surprise, this calling to open up a homeless shelter took over my being. I prayed to Jesus to take this opportunity away if it wasn't His plan, because I didn't think I could say no if it was offered. Each time I prayed that, my passion increased, so I knew God was once again calling me to action!

I accepted this position and dove into what became the greatest mission of my life. Instantly, miracles started pouring down on us as we were hit with many challenges. An example of this was opening the shelter six days after I started, six months early! I didn't even have a plan or staff, and our building was under construction with no heat, hot water, or proper space! But when the temperatures dropped to single digits and an abandoned house burned down in town, putting ten homeless folks on the streets with only the shirts on their back in six-degree temps, how do you ignore that? You don't! But God hung in there with us. He sent the right people and plenty of donations to make it work every day! It was incredible to experience.

Then, 2 ½ months later, we had a team and settled into a grove, and BAM, we got hit with a global pandemic that sent us all into a frenzy to protect the homeless and the rest of the community! We had to shut down our makeshift shelter and work from the parking lot and our cars. BUT God is good, and every issue seemed to work itself out seamlessly and even put the agency in a better place. We received un-expected funding–more than a new agency deserves, and the right people with the hugest hearts always showed up at just the right time!

> For I know the thoughts that I think toward you, saith the LORD, thoughts of peace, and not of evil, to give you an expected end. Then call ye call upon me, and ye shall go and pray unto me, and I will hearken unto you. And ye shall seek me, and find me, when ye shall search for me with all your heart, And I will be found of you, saith the LORD: and I will turn away your captivity, and I will gather you from all the nations, and from all the places whither I have driven you, saith the LORD; and I will bring you again into the place whence I caused you to be carried away captive (Jeremiah 29:11-14).

About four months into this chaos, I suddenly remem-bered the business plan that I had tucked away. It stopped me cold in my tracks as I realized God was watching all along, preparing me for this mission. Maybe this is why God called me to NM and blessed me with this magical life-style.

Helping to start this agency and serve this community was the greatest honor of my life. It was God's work like I had never experienced. I met a community with a heart that was impressive and humbling. And thanks to a team of warriors, we created a foundation of multiple critical services this area desperately needed and served almost 2,000 people. Mission accomplished.

Two years later, God sent another message: "Time to prepare for the next mission. Leave the agency now, or you will not be ready for what's coming." This came about suddenly, and at first, I felt unready to leave. It took me a month to justify it in my mind professionally. I was afraid to leave too soon. But the moment I surrendered to it, I realized my mission was indeed accomplished; the organization was stable and getting ready to enter a new phase. It was, in fact, the best time to move on.

Here we go again!

The day after I resigned, I had a dream showing me that I would write another book. It woke me up suddenly, in a state of shock. I retired from writing books ten years prior, so I wasn't interested in writing another. I resisted the idea, asking God, "Do I really have to?" Well, it only took moments to realize that God was revealing his next plan for me. "OK," I said, "I will write another book, and I'm sure when you are ready, you will reveal the topic!" Then I went back to sleep.

The next night, I dreamt about the topic, and on the third night, God revealed the entire outline for this book in my dream.

And here we are!

Anyone that knows me knows I do not believe in coincidences. It's obvious to me that God is at work here, and this book is a product of that.

This book is meant for you to think about your own callings. When has God talked to you or guided you? Did you know it was God, or did you think it was your imagination? Did you follow? If so, how did it change your life? Did you take all the credit or give it to God? Or are you wondering why you cannot hear God talking to you? Read on to learn about true life examples from other s who have received God's messages when they least expected it. But they followed, and you'll see how their worlds changed! You just might be amazed!

Part 2:
Shared Experiences
by
the Contribution Team

Chapter 3

God Rescued Me from Addiction & Changed My Entire Being

By Shannon Baum

When I was a child, I did not look forward to going to church and Saturday studies. I wanted to be outside and play with the neighborhood kids. My life was not what I felt was normal. Most kids my age didn't know the stories of the Bible. Most of my friends knew of Jesus, but they did not really know about him or about God. They just knew what the Priest taught, which seemed redundant every Sunday at the local church. Sing hymns, stand when everyone else does, sit when others sit, repeat prayer, and kneel for communion. It was the same every Sunday. This was where my life differed from others. My Mom started following the instructions of the Bible, which differed from what was the norm in my town.

When we began attending church on Saturday, people looked at us differently. My friends thought I was weird. My mom would not allow a Christmas tree in our house, and the coloring of eggs was not celebrated after a while either. I was only eight years old, and this felt like God was punishing me because my mom said God doesn't allow it. It sounded like she blamed God for not having a Christmas tree. But everyone had a Christmas tree, and I felt like an outcast. I felt like I was missing out on all the fun that everyone else was having. I watched others have family celebrations. I felt bad thinking I'll never have that. Plus, some family members yelled at my mom, calling her selfish. That made me feel unloved. I couldn't help but wonder *why she was punishing me.*

This continued as I grew up. While attending a public school, I couldn't participate in school activities because I had to worship. Anything I did participate in was done without family support because I was doing what my parents said wasn't allowed. They weren't there to cheer me on in sports. I felt so alone and unloved. In my teenage years, I rebelled a lot more than a normal teenager. As soon as I was old enough to get a little freedom, I turned to the first things I could: drugs, boys, and alcohol, because I was starving for attention and support. I, for once, craved to be the center of attention. My parents were always upset with me and didn't know how to handle me. My mom cried and prayed a lot, and my dad tried to strong-arm me into being obedient. But punishment and guilt made me feel worse. In fact, I left home altogether by sixteen and got caught up in drugs, alcohol, and the world's enticements. But ultimately, this was not fulfilling at all. Over many years, I made a complete mess of my life and found myself in utter brokenness. Not only did I destroy my life, but I also abandoned my family and left a trail of destruction in the lives of those that loved me.

They say that the path of drugs and alcohol will either take you to prison or to your grave. They were right. As I lay in a jail cell on a cold floor in a puddle of my tears, I thought about what I had become, and the shame and guilt engulfed me. I wanted to die. I didn't know how to face these things I had done.

The previous night: I woke up in the hospital after hitting a boy on a motorcycle. I was intoxicated and very high on drugs. The officer sitting by my bedside said, "Good thing you're awake because I don't think the kid you hit is going to make it through the night. He's in ICU right now, fighting for his life." I just wanted to die. At that moment, pure madness overcame me, and I reached for the officer's gun because I wanted to shoot myself and die before any more time went by. I couldn't bear what I was feeling. I went into such a frenzy that they had to sedate me. That made me feel like a zombie. Once the exam was over, I was transported to the local jail.

In desperation, I called out to God that night and throughout the day, begging for help. I bargained with everything I had, including my children.

I will call upon the Lord, who is worthy to be praised: So shall I be saved from mine enemies (Psalm 18:3).

That next evening, Jesus answered my prayers. In fact, what was done was nothing short of a miracle. He saved the life of the young man I hit on a motorcycle. I was going 70 mph. It had to have been God who saved him.

From that moment, I knew God heard my cries, and it was now my move. For the first time, as I was coming down from drugs and alcohol, I felt a fear of God that was so strong. I knew I could not fall back into the sin of using drugs because the repercussions would be a death of those I held dearest to my heart: my children. That fear kept me strong throughout the initial sickness of detox. I kept thinking, "Oh my Gosh, he heard me. Me! After everything I've done, he heard ME! He's really there! He is real! He knows who I am." That was a life-changing moment. I knew now I had to live up to my bargain.

Then shall ye call upon me, and ye shall go and pray unto me, and I will hearken unto you. And ye shall seek me and find me, when ye shall search for me with all your heart (Jeremiah 29:12-13).

I ended up serving two years on a four-year judgment in prison. During this time, my walk with God flourished. My walk with God began with the fear of God because I knew God could do anything, which scared me. I knew he could see my every action and my every thought. I needed to change my life, or I would fall into that trap again. So, I started reading my Bible, praying, and singing songs of praise every day. Soon after, I noticed that other women at the prison wanted to participate in Bible study. They wanted to know more about God. Before I knew it, the whole pod began praying and singing songs of praise before bed each night. Soon, it spread to the other pods in the jail.

This was such a crazy and incredible experience! Such an amazing feeling to know that this was touching people's hearts. I didn't want to take the credit. I knew God used me to help the other girls see that good things start to happen when you turn your heart to God. The guards stopped punishing the girls. There were no more lockdowns and they stopped taking privileges away. What I realized is that it was because the fighting stopped and everyone was suddenly getting along. There was no more gossip, and the anger, revenge and bitterness had decreased drastically. The presence of the Lord was there so there was less sin, more happiness. Others started learning that when they pray, they get blessings from God. Then other pods started praying because they wanted God's blessings. And even though they weren't perfect, God still honored their efforts to praise him. It was contagious!

Be careful for nothing; but in every thing by prayer and supplication with thanksgiving let your requests

be made known unto God. And the peace of God, which passeth all understanding, shall keep your hearts and minds through Christ Jesus. (Philippians 4:6-7)

As I grew closer to Jesus, reading his word and what he had sacrificed for me, I fell in love with my father in heaven. The fear subsided, but I still knew that God was the King of the Universe and could do anything, but he's not about fear. He is about love, and there is nothing to be afraid of. I also learned that I needed that fear to get clean and sober. Jesus led me down the path of the valley of fear to get me to unconditional love. As that happened to me, the love I felt for my Jesus became overwhelmingly wonderful. I wanted to do what he asked of me to show him how much I loved him.

During the early days of my walk with God, he revealed gifts he had blessed me with through visions that would actually come to pass. One of my first visions came to me while still in the county jail, awaiting my sentence. God showed me the consequences of unrighteous anger, which I was filled with at the time. Here's what happened:

In jail, I was known as the mom, and the others came to me for guidance. I'll never forget; one of the girls came to me several times after another inmate took advantage of her. It infuriated me because she kept doing the same thing that caused her to get ripped off. After a while, I asked her not to tell me about it anymore, but she continued. That triggered me. I lost control and yelled at her severely. After that, the other girls ganged up on her often because they didn't like that she made me angry. They were showing their loyalty to me! After a few days, I woke up scared in the middle of the night. I saw a black shadow against the wall that kept getting closer, and a horrible feeling overcame me. Soon, the shadow felt like it was on top of me. I wondered, *why is this happening to me?* What did I do to deserve this? I asked God, "Why are you doing this to me?" I kept asking and asking and feared God wasn't listening to me. And then suddenly, I experienced what felt like a telepathic download that I couldn't put into words. It was like a tidal wave of information that came over me. I didn't hear anything. It just was there. And this is what it was:

"I didn't do this to you. You did this to yourself. You opened the door and let it in with your unrighteous anger. How dare you speak to a child of mine like that!"

At that point, I knew it was God, and I fell to my knees and begged for forgiveness. And then, that evil feeling that was overtaking me was completely gone. I started thanking God. Then, I heard,

"You WILL go to prison, and it will be my training ground for you. I am preparing you for what is to

43

come."

After that, I had a vision of women/mothers, all in black, sitting in front of a Walgreens pharmacy in our town. They were holding their dead sons, crying over their bodies. Then it all ended. I couldn't sleep after that. It was about 3 am. At daybreak, I went up to the girl I had yelled at, and, in front of everyone else, I broke down and apologized to her. She broke down also, and we hugged, and the situation dissipated. Just like that! Soon after, I was transferred to prison. What I heard that night came to life, and it certainly was a life-changing calling.

While in prison, I started attending church and attending every meeting about God. This led to meeting like-minded women who wanted to serve the Lord. I began building friendships with some of them. One woman stood out. She was from my hometown, and her brother was one of my good friends in high school. We hit it off instantly, and she became one of my best friends. One day, she approached me and asked if I wanted to do an ordination program. She explained that it was a 6-12-month program of intense study of the Bible. There are over 2,000 questions on the books of the Bible at the end of the course. We would then receive certificates as ordained ministers to preach the word of God. I looked at her as if she were crazy and said, "ME a minister? You know how ridiculous that sounds? God doesn't want me as a minster! You know the things

I've done. How could I be a minister with a past like mine?" And I laughed at her.

Soon after, I started helping the other girls study for this ordination. I did this just to help them because, in my mind, I believed I wasn't worthy of such an honor. I thought it was crazy; who becomes ordained in prison? God doesn't want us felons as pastors!! How could anyone think they'd be accepted after all they've done? It made me laugh!! BUT as time went on, I did the course myself for the sole purpose of learning. I thought more knowledge and a certificate would help me get work later, but I never intended to minister! Before long, the others fell away from the program. They got distracted, or they just got tired of doing it. I enjoyed the program, and it became a personal goal to complete the course in six months, no longer. The six months came, and during the last hour of the last day of the six months, I finished it. I was so happy! I took my packet of papers with all my answers to my pastor with boundless joy and turned it in for review.

Eventually, I received my certificate of ordination. And, oh my, from that point, I started praying with others; I preached to other women and held classes on life recovery through the Bible. I worked at the church in the prison and ministered to the girls that came in for prayer or were looking for God. I felt the need to get up and tell people about God; in fact, it was so strong that I asked the pastor if

I could lead the Sunday service! He agreed to allow me one Sunday.

On that Sunday morning, I was excited and nervous all at the same time. When I got up there, I knew that this was what God had called me to do — to spread the Gospel, tell others of his goodness and mercy through my testimony, and give God the glory. From that point on, I continued preaching every chance I got.

And Jesus came and spake unto them, saying All power is given unto me in heaven and in earth. Go ye therefore, and teach all nations, baptizing them in the name of the Father, and of the Son, and of the Holy Ghost: teaching them to observe all things whatsoever I have commanded you: and, lo, I am with you always, even unto the end the world. Amen (Matthew 28:18-20).

When I got out of prison, I did not know where God would use me, but I knew he had a plan. I had a strong desire to help the homeless, so the first month out of jail, my cousin Nicole and I made snack packs for the homeless and put little notes with scriptures inside them. We also handed out blankets and clothes as we preached the good news of the Gospel, giving hope and encouragement to them. During my 2nd month out of prison (January 2020), God opened the door for me to be the manager of the first homeless shelter in Española. It is a town in northern New

Mexico that suffers from poverty, generational addiction, and homelessness. It is also where I grew up. Working with those suffering from drugs and alcohol addiction and telling them the way out through Jesus has been a privilege I never imagined I'd be worthy of! During my 3rd month out of prison, I began teaching a Life Recovery Bible course that still exists today, at The Rock Church in Española, for anyone suffering from addiction or life's hardships. After 3 years of managing the homeless shelter, I moved on to become the Justice Program Advocate for the Office of Peer Recovery and Engagement (OPRE).

I have been out of prison since November 2019 and clean and sober since 2017! During this time, God has been placing me in environments where I could help those struggling with many things that I struggled with. He has me working in the same community where I burned bridges during my addiction. I now work hand-in-hand with law enforcement and other leaders I once fought against! God has renewed my heart to see the tremendous value the police and others bring to a community. God has restored my reputation in a community that once frowned upon me. God also restored my relationship with my mom and dad, and now we serve God in one accord. And recently, with the power of the Holy Spirit guiding me, I have written a book titled *Breaking the Chains.* I intend to use this book to reach many more across the globe, hoping to show people the power of Jesus because, through Him, we can have victory over our lives.

God calls us all to be his children through his son Jesus. We can call ourselves children of God by having faith and ministering the word to others. Without faith, our works are futile. We must come into conjunction with our faith with good works. This is what the calling of God is.

God gave me other gifts, which I explain in detail in my book *Breaking the Chains*.

Shannon Baum is the Justice Program Advocate for OPRE in New Mexico. She is also an ordained Minister, founder/leader of a Christian AA/NA group, Bible Study leader, and author of *Breaking the Chains*, which is also the name of her new ministry. http://www.BreakingtheChainsMinistry.com Shannon can be reached at 505-990-9086 or BreakingtheChains505@gmail.com

Chapter 4

God Called Me for HIS Purpose

By James J. Martinez

It was the spring of 1976; a young couple was expecting their second child, praying for a son. Their firstborn was a girl, and a boy would be an answer to prayer. Then it happened. I was born on May 6, 1976, in Española, NM. God had answered their prayer. A seemingly healthy baby boy until, two months later, that day came.

It was at a routine well-baby check-up that the doctor knew something wasn't right with one of my kidneys. After further medical tests, the doctors told my parents that my left kidney needed to be surgically removed. But, as I was still an infant, the doctors recommended that they wait until I was a year old to do the surgery. During the next several months, I learned to crawl, walk, talk, and do most everything a baby of that age would do. My parents continued to pray and ask for God's protection upon their baby boy.

It was the day of the surgery, and the doctors told my parents there was a 50% chance that I would survive the operation. My parents asked God for protection. They believed that God would watch over their son as he went into that operating room. They believed that God had more life for their son to live.

And so that serves as confirmation that since long ago, God called me for His purpose.

Before I formed thee in the belly I knew thee; and before thou camest forthout of the womb I sanctified thee, and I ordained thee a prophet unto the nations (Jeremiah 1:5).

I was raised in a Christian home and learned from my parents the importance of having a relationship with Jesus, prioritizing church, helping others, working hard, and valuing education. I saw my parents volunteer at our church and do their part to help in ministry. I always knew that I would contribute to my local church somehow, but as a child, I didn't know exactly how.

When I became a teenager, church wasn't as appealing. I seemed to always "miss out" on the school games and hanging out with friends because I had to be in church. I met a girl from school. We got to know each other when she and I worked at the same grocery store. Her dad was a pastor at a local Christian church. She became the positive influence I needed in my life again. I graduated from high school and left home to attend college. I was excited about the freedom I would have and being able to make my own choices. Even during that time, I didn't feel comfortable hanging out with friends, doing my own thing. I knew there had to be more to life than this. I continued to go back to my parents' home on weekends, spend time with my girlfriend, and attend our local church. We got married, and then I really got serious about serving God, reading the Bible more, and volunteering at our church. God had been working on me, and I knew He was leading me into more ministry.

In 1999, I was asked to speak at our church. This would be the first time I would share a sermon in front of a large group. As I prayed and studied scripture, God impressed different verses on my heart and mind, confirming the message I was to share. Although I knew God had given me the words to say, I remember how uncomfortable I was as I stood in front of the church and tried to articulate an encouraging yet challenging message. As I spoke, I recognized God speaking through me. After the sermon, I knew that this was something God had called me to do. From that moment on, I began to dig deeper into the Bible. I balanced my college studies with Bible studies and prayer, which focused on asking God to continue to guide and use me for His work.

The years went on. More opportunities became available to volunteer at our local church, to show the love of Jesus, and to share my faith with others. I still had this desire to teach the Word of God. I would read scripture and write notes and outlines for sermons. I listened to Bible teachers on the radio. I attended evangelistic crusades and revival meetings. I read Christian-based books. I consistently fed myself the Word of God and learned more, asking God for new revelation and insight. Even though I was raised in a Christian home and went to church regularly, much of what I was reading and learning was fresh and became alive within my heart and mind. As I look back at those years, I see how God was preparing me for what He had planned for me in the future.

In 2001, I graduated with my master's degree from the university. It was time to go back home. My wife and I had always planned to return to our hometown after college to work, raise our daughters, and help our home church in any way we could. I had grown up in a Christian church down the road from my wife's home church. Her dad was a pastor and had founded their church in the 1980s. It was a growing church with volunteers doing most of the work of the ministry. After prayer and godly counsel, my wife and I made "her" home church "our" church. And we have been a part of it ever since.

Looking back, I had such a positive experience growing up in church. As a youth, I moved from knowing who God is to a place where I came to know Jesus as my personal Lord and Savior. At a young age, I knew God had called me to contribute to our local ministry. My wife knew God had called her to the work of the ministry. We knew that together, as a married couple and as a family, along with our daughters, we were called to contribute to the work of our local church.

The Bible reminds us in the New Testament Book of 1 Corinthians that, as Christian believers, we are all called to contribute to the work of God. The Bible compares the church to a physical body, where each part has a responsibility and a role. And each part adds to the body's overall function. In the same way, the church is made up of various "parts," and each part contributes to the overall function of the church. Each of us has a responsibility and a role. We are all called to be participants and not just spectators.

As a young adult, I realized that just because my parents were Christians didn't mean that I would automatically be a Christian and follow Jesus. I was not guaranteed to continue attending church and living for God. God doesn't have *grandchildren*, just *children*. Each of us as individuals must realize we are sinners and recognize that we need a Savior. I came to that place early in life. I certainly haven't lived my life perfectly, but I always knew God had a purpose for me to fulfill.

I continued to volunteer at our church in any way I could. I would usher and greet church members and visitors during church services. I participated in church clean-up and fundraiser events. I remained in Bible study, prayer, reading Christian books, and attending evangelistic and revival meetings. The church leadership took notice of my willingness to help. I was then asked to teach a small group Bible study as part of our church discipleship program.

After years of teaching Bible studies, hosting a small group at our home, volunteering for church clean-up days, ushering, fundraising, distributing food to the needy, sharing my faith with others—everything done with faithfulness, not expecting anything in return—in 2005, our senior pastor offered me a promotion as associate pastor of our local church. The first thoughts that came to mind were, I'm not ready; I don't know how to be a pastor; I don't have any credentials, training, or education. Thoughts of inadequacy—I'm unworthy and unprepared—flooded my mind. When God calls, it's sometimes to an area or a position that is scary, uncomfortable, or uncertain. That's when we need to trust God and take a step of faith, to believe and trust that God is in control and that God does everything for our good and for our benefit. Through prayer, fasting, and seeking confirmation from God, I humbly accepted the associate pastor position.

Since 2005, I have served as associate pastor of the Rock Christian Fellowship Church in Española, NM. I continue to lead Bible studies, preach sermons, minister, facilitate our Bible College program, and coordinate and support outreach, food distribution, and fundraising events. Other pastoral duties include officiating wedding ceremonies,

baby and child dedications, water baptisms, funeral services, and other ministry responsibilities. I am thankful that
God called me to the work of the ministry. I ask God for
the strength, wisdom, energy, good health, creativity, and
opportunities to continue fulfilling His purpose for my life.

ᏑᏑᏑᏑ

James J. Martinez, A.B.S., B.T., M.T. (in progress)
is a husband, dad, school staff member, state-
licensed, nationally certified therapist, and County
Commissioner.
He is also the Associate Pastor at:
Rock Christian Fellowship
919 N. Riverside Drive
Española, NM 87532
Ph. 505-927-2055
Jamesmartinez91@gmail.com

Chapter 5

God Paved My Path Out of Homelessness

By Ralph Martinez

Living homeless is far from easy. There are many luxuries a homeless person does not have. Here's my story of coming out of homelessness.

My name is Ralph Martinez, and I was born and raised in the beautiful Española Valley. I graduated from Española Valley High in 1996. After graduation, I settled down and started a family with my high school sweetheart. At the time, my high school sweetheart was already blessed with two small children. I hold those children close to my heart as my own. We were able to secure a home in Velarde, New Mexico, where we began life as a family.

In 2001, I became addicted to drugs, cocaine, and heroin, to be exact. This addiction made life very hard for us. It got to a point where I couldn't hold a job, and all the pressures of life were falling into the hands of my high school sweetheart. In 2003, we had another child of our own. That put us at three children … as my addiction grew.

In 2006, my high school sweetheart couldn't take my

addiction problem any longer. I don't blame her, as I was creating many difficulties for our family. She asked me to leave. I lost everything that year—my family, home, and self-identity. I ended up homeless in my community. I lived homeless for six years as my addiction grew out of control. During this time, I lived in makeshift tents in empty fields and abandoned buildings, seeking shelter wherever I could, depending on the time of year. I often went months without a shower, brushing my teeth, or even changing clothes. This way of life helped to fuel my addiction as the depression of life grew.

In 2009, I had a makeshift tent in the back of an empty field. The makeshift tent consisted of two big bushes next to each other, with old blankets draped over the top of both bushes that acted as a rooftop. Between the bushes, more old blankets made up a bedlike resting spot. One night during monsoon season, I was curled up in a ball between the bushes on the bed-like ground as torrential rain poured down on me. I was getting drenched as it rained uncontrollably. I remember crying as I contemplated what to do with my life. I asked God why I had to be in the position I was in. As many thoughts flowed through my mind, a small voice spoke to my soul. The voice said, "Hold on to hope, as I have bigger plans for you." I didn't know what that meant at the time, but I heard it loud and clear.

In 2012, after two overdoses, six rehab attempts, and

many times incarcerated, I was blessed to plant my feet back on the ground and begin a strong recovery. This recovery was built on a foundation of many lessons learned and many acceptances I was able to come to. I accepted that I was different from others, and that was okay because we are all different. Those differences are what make us all unique. I accepted that boundary lines in my life needed to exist, and that was okay because boundary lines keep us on track. I accepted that life wasn't a race, as I often felt behind in the race of life, and I accepted that I still had life to live. These acceptances were huge for me.

In November 2018, after being clean and sober for six years, I stopped by Walmart one night to get lunch items for the week. I felt the cold weather hit my skin as I got out of my vehicle. I reached into the back seat to get my jacket. As I walked toward the front door of the Walmart, I noticed three homeless individuals sitting on a curb next to the entrance of the store. It made me think of the cold nights I spent when I was homeless and what it took to survive all that. When I got to the front door, I stopped to talk to these three individuals. I knew them all by name. One individual and I shared space at one point when I was homeless. I asked them if they were prepared for the winter season that was coming up. We spoke about what it took to stay safe while being homeless during the winter season. I shared with them a story about things I did to stay warm during the winter while I was homeless. We spoke like old friends for 45 minutes before I said goodbye and proceeded with my shopping.

When I got home that night and lay in bed, I couldn't stop thinking about my conversation with the three homeless individuals. It made me think of what my community was lacking in support of the homeless situation. I thought about the different needs a person living homeless had during each season. I started thinking about what they could benefit from. *Shelter.* At that time, there was no homeless shelter, and there had never been a shelter in my community. A voice spoke to my soul, saying, "Make the call." Not really understanding what "Make the call" really meant, my heart instructed me to put together a text message explaining the encounter I just had with the three homeless individuals, how I related to all they were going through, and the much-needed supportive services our community lacked for individuals down on their luck. At that time, I was blessed to have built a network of city, county, state, judicial, faith-based, and organizational leaders. I obeyed the command given to my heart and put together a lengthy text message to all these leaders in my community. When I finally finished typing, it was a little past 1 am. I thought about waiting to send the message but was spiritually influenced to hit the send button right then and there. And so, I did!

That text message opened the door to conversations that

led to multiple actions spiraling into a community coming together for the well-being of the homeless. Because of that voice and the seed planted in my heart to send that text message, the very first homeless shelter was born in my community. The Española Pathways Shelter now serves my community's most vulnerable in many capacities. Within two years, we were blessed with the ability to open the doors to a facility and gain the financial support of $250,000 in recurring funds through State Legislation for operations, as well as almost $500,000 in COVID relief funds to purchase an old motel across the street from Española Pathways Shelter. That motel was transformed into Española's first transitional housing program. It was most recently granted $1.89 million to acquire the building and property, catapulting our efforts to serve the less fortunate from a self-sustainability standpoint.

I give all credit to God, who paved the way and made it all possible through His voice of guidance.

With Him are wisdom and strength, He has counsel and understanding (Job 12:13 NKJV).

And in the wilderness where you saw how the Lord your God carried you, as a man carries his son, in all the way that you went until you came to this place (Deuteronomy 1:31 NKJV).

ᏄᏄᏄ

Ralph Martinez is a Co-Founder and former
Board President of the Española Pathways
Shelter in Española, New Mexico. He works as
a Government Affairs Specialist at Los Alamos
National Laboratory. Ralph cares deeply about
his community and is genuinely grateful for the
support he has received. He remains extremely
active in giving back and serving the area in
multiple ways.

RJMarti35@gmail.com

505-221-3227.

Chapter 6

Getting "Saved" Shows Up in Many Ways

By Diana Baum

- God Rescued Me from Rape
- We Argued Over Tithes & God Provided
- What is the True Religion?
- Jesus Saved My Son and Me from a Horrific Death

As a child, I was raised Catholic, which my mother made sure of. My dad stood over our beds every night when we were little to ensure we said our prayers. He always told me, "Don't be afraid of the devil. God is more powerful. Just pray the Our Father and trust God, and He will help you." I remembered that always. It saved me so many times that it would take a very long book to tell all the stories of my Father in heaven and His saving grace in my life. Here, I'd like to share a few of the most impactful memories of where God came to me and saved me through dreams and His guidance.

God Rescued Me from Rape

It was a night I'll never forget. I was at a party with several friends. I was about fifteen years old. The house was filled with loud music, lots of drinking, smoking, and noise. One of the girls announced to everyone that she could chug a 5th of tequila, which sent everyone in cheers and inspired an alcohol run to a bar about three miles away. An older guy around nineteen or so offered to go pick it up, but he wanted me to go with him. I was uncomfortable with that and refused since I didn't know him. One of my best friends told me to go with him because he was a friend of her sister's, so he was trustworthy. I still refused, but he said he wouldn't go unless I went. My friend convinced me that he was a nice guy. Plus, he had a '57 Chevy with tuck and roll, a great stereo with great headphones; so, being a vulnerable teen under peer pressure, I finally agreed to go.

I got in the front passenger seat, put on his headphones, then closed my eyes for the ride to the bar. I was really enjoying the music with my head back, eyes shut, when it suddenly felt like we were on a bumpy road, and I thought, "there are no bumpy roads on the way to this bar"! I instantly opened my eyes and was shocked to see that he had driven us down a dirt road in the middle of nowhere. When I asked him where we were, he replied, "Oh, we're just going to look at the view." At this point, I started to get really scared. My fifteen-year-old virgin heart began pounding, and I felt like I was going to hyperventilate. My mouth was so dry from fear.

He stopped the car, pushed me down on the seat, and climbed on me. I tried to fight him off. Scared for my life, I grabbed his throat around the windpipe and squeezed as hard as I could. He couldn't breathe and was gasping for air. I realized I might be close to killing him, so I let go. At this point, he's now fuming and pulled out a pocketknife, then put it to my throat. He ordered me to take off my shirt. I took it off and grabbed the steering wheel, thinking that if I just held on tight, he couldn't take off my pants in this sitting position.

As I struggled to fight him off and keep him from taking my pants off, I prayed, "Oh, God, please help me. I promise I will never get in a car with someone I don't know again. Just please help me, Lord." Suddenly, I heard in my mind, "Tell him you love him." That made no sense to me!! I thought, *What?* But I was out of choices, and my life was in danger, so, obediently through my tears, I said to him, "I love you; why are you trying to hurt me?" At that moment, he came out of the trance he seemed to be in and stopped wrestling with me. He just looked at me and said, "I'm sorry, so sorry." He then handed me my shirt and took me back to the party.

I walked in with my shirt on backward, and my best

friend gave me that "look" as if he and I had something going on. I told her it was not what she was thinking and showed her the bruises on my stomach from clinging to the steering wheel so tightly. I later found out that this guy had been involved in a stabbing just weeks before this. I knew God heard me and saved me. God delivered me from evil. My Deliverer.

> **Fear not, for I am with you; Be not dismayed, for I am your God. I will strengthen you, Yes, I will help you, I will uphold you with My righteous right hand (Isaiah 41:10 NKJV).**

> **But I say to you, love your enemies, bless those who curse you, do good to those who hate you, and pray for those who spitefully use you and persecute you (Matthew 5:44 NKJV).**

> **Beloved, do not avenge yourselves, but rather give place to wrath; for it is written, "Vengeance is Mine, I will repay," says the Lord (Romans 12:19 NKJV).**

We Argued Over Tithes, and God Provided

When I read Malachi Chapter 3 in the Bible, it helped me understand a little bit about the law of tithing. So, I decided my husband Billy and I would pay tithes. But there was another reason for paying tithes and trusting God to provide: to prove my love for God.

Billy and I argued for months over this. He argued that we needed to buy a car since ours was breaking down; therefore, we could not afford to pay tithes. I argued back that if we needed a car, God would provide. I negotiated with Billy by saying to him, "Don't buy me anything, no clothes, no shoes, no jewelry, etc. Let it go to tithes." As the months went by, we continued to argue about this, but Billy usually goes along even though he complains! One day, during the Christmas holiday, a brand-new Ford Ranger was delivered to our home. *Seriously!* There was a knock at the door in the morning while we were still in bed. I got up to answer, and they handed me the keys to a new vehicle. I said, "No, there has been a mistake. We didn't order a vehicle, nor do we have the money to pay for one. Please take it back.

They asked, "Is this the residence of Billy Baum?"

"Yes!" I answered.

They replied, "It's yours. Merry Christmas!"

I called the Ford dealership to explain there was a mistake, and they assured me it was not. I ran to the bedroom and gave the keys to Billy, and, seeing God's blessing, I said, "I told you if God thought we needed a car, he would give us one." Billy and the kids jumped out of bed and took it for a test drive to my Dad's because all year, he agreed with Billy about us being unable to afford to tithe! My Dad and everyone were in awe! God is sooo good. And God continued to open doors for us throughout our lives. Billy has never complained about giving the tithe after that. He became a believer.

As it turned out, Billy's grandpa had the truck delivered to us. I believe God moved his heart as God does in many stories of the Bible. I believe that because Billy's grandfather had twelve other grandkids, and we got to be the ones he gifted with the truck the very same year we began tithing. Yahweh, God, our Father, truly opened the windows of Heaven for us. He is a trustworthy and amazing Father.

And this stone which I have set for a pillar, shall be God's house: and of all that Thou shalt give me I will surely give a tenth unto Thee (Genesis 28:22).

Bring ye all the tithes into the storehouse, that there may be meat in mine house, and prove me now herewith, saith the LORD of hosts, if I will not open you the windows of heaven, and pour you out a blessing, that there shall not be room enough to receive it (Malachi 3:10).

What is the True Religion?

When I was a teenager visiting my aunt in Los Angeles, we were walking downtown. The streets were full of people walking, shopping, selling, smoking pot, and doing drugs. This was in the '70s, the time of drugs, sex, rock & roll, hippies, and "Jesus Freaks" (that is what they called people sharing the Gospel then). One of them approached me and handed me a New Testament Bible. I read it and was fascinated by the book of Revelation. It stayed in my heart.

When I was about eighteen and pregnant with my daughter Shannon, I read the Bible cover to cover but was too busy being a new mom to focus on God. A few years later, my son Adam was born, and I began reading the Bible more often. I searched for the "right" way to worship God. I discovered the Worldwide Church of God teachings about the Sabbath Day. I studied with Jehovah's Witnesses and Mormons. As time went on, I got very confused, wondering which really were the true teachings. I decided to pray and fast. I prayed something like this: "Lord, all these religions claim they are the true religion. Please, Father, tell me which one is the true religion?"

I had a dream a couple of days later that went like this:

I was in the kitchen at my maternal grandma's house, frantically searching the scriptures to find eternal life. I kept looking out the window because I knew it would be too late to find eternal life when the sun went down. Right before sunset, an older man of small stature with long graying hair and a beard came into the house, and I knew it was Isaiah the Prophet. His eyes were piercing, and he looked right into my eyes, right into my soul. He pointed

68

his finger at me and said, "Be for me or against me!" He walked out the southern door and left the door cracked slightly open. An extremely bright light shone through the crack of the door like brilliant sunlight.

Then I woke up, and Isaiah 57 came to my mind. So, I ran to find a Bible and opened to Isaiah 57, looking for a connection to the dream, but I didn't find any. Continuing to Isaiah 58, I was stunned to see the title "Fasting that Pleases God." It reminded me of my prayer a couple days prior, where I had asked the Lord about which was the true religion. In his wonderful mercy, lovingkindness, and amazing grace, he answered my prayer! It is copied here:

Fasting that Pleases God

"Cry aloud, spare not; Lift up your voice like a trumpet; Tell My people their transgression, And the house of Jacob their sins. Yet they seek Me daily, And delight to know My ways, As a nation that did righteousness, And did not forsake the ordinance of their God. They ask of Me the ordinances of justice; They take delight in approaching God. 'Why have we fasted,' they say, 'and You have not seen? Why have we afflicted our souls, and You take no notice?' In fact, in the day of your fast you find pleasure, And exploit all your laborers. Indeed you fast for strife and debate, and to strike with the fist of wickedness.

You will not fast as you do this day, To make your voice heard on high. Is it a fast that I have chosen, A day for a man to afflict his soul? Is it to bow down his head like a bulrush, And to spread out sackcloth and ashes? Would you call this a fast, And an acceptable day to the Lord. "Is this not the fast that I have chosen: To loose the bonds of wickedness, To undo the heavy burdens, To let the oppressed go free, And that you break every yoke? Is it not to share your bread with the hungry, And that you bring to your house the poor who are cast out; When you see the naked, that you cover him, And not hide yourself from your own flesh? Then your light shall break forth like the morning, Your healing shall spring forth speedily, And your righteousness shall go before you; The glory of the Lord shall be your rear guard. Then you shall call, and the Lord will answer; You shall cry, and He will say, 'Here I am.' If you take away the yoke from your midst, The pointing of the finger, and speaking wickedness, If you extend your soul to the hungry And satisfy the afflicted soul, Then your light shall dawn in the darkness, And your darkness shall be as the noonday. The Lord will guide you continually, And satisfy your soul in drought, And strengthen your bones; You shall be like a watered garden, And like a spring of water, whose waters do not fail. Those from among you Shall build the old waste places; You shall raise up the foundations of many generations; And you shall be called the Repairer of the Breach, The Restorer of Streets to Dwell In. If you turn away your foot from the Sabbath, From doing your pleasure on My holy day, And call the Sabbath a delight, The holy day of the Lord honorable, And shall honor Him, not doing your own ways, Nor finding your own pleasure, Nor speaking your own words, Then you shall delight yourself in the Lord; And I will cause you to ride on the high hills of the earth, And feed you with the heritage of Jacob your father. The mouth of the Lord has spoken (Isaiah 58 NKJV).

Now that I knew and understood what true religion was, I realized I must practice His instructions as instructed in Isaiah 58. It wasn't easy at first, but as time went on, my family supported me, and God has been with me, guiding me ever since.

This dream blew my mind:

I was climbing a mountain, and the closer I got to the top, the harder I struggled. I slid back many times. A few times, it seemed like I slid all the way to the bottom, but I knew I had to get over the mountain because there was something there. So, I kept trying to reach the top and get over the mountain. It was so hard. I was struggling, tired, and sweating, but I knew I had to climb that mountain. Finally, after struggling so hard, I reached the top and made it over to the other side. I stood dressed in white, with no makeup, standing in the very presence of God Almighty! There was such a wonderful sense of peace, joy, and well-being. Something so wonderful, so amazing, and marvelous; there aren't any words in the English language to describe that awesome feeling. To this day, I have not found the words. When I awoke from that dream, I woke up my husband and told him all about it but couldn't find words or ways to describe the feeling of being in the presence of God. For lack of a way to help him understand, I said something like, "It was so awesome, like nothing on this earth! Better than sex!" Then I told him, "I want to be with God no matter what it costs me!"

That dream changed my life. I decided that night that I would give my heart and soul and all that I had, including my life, if that is what it takes, to be in the presence of My Good God Almighty, My Creator, my Savior, my Protector. He is literally the air that I breathe! Yet as much as I want that, I still pray that I will have the love, faith, and courage to stand my ground for God my Father (Abba Yah) and Jesus (Yeshua, my Salvation), whatever the cost. This prayer is for my husband, children, mom, dad, grandchildren, and all my family and friends. May all our names be written in the Lamb's book of Life; may we all choose Life.

Jesus Saved My Son and Me from a Horrific Death

I was in the car with my son Adam, who was only three years old. We were stopped at an intersection on the highway, waiting to make a turn. I glanced in the rear-view mirror and saw an SUV traveling at an extremely high speed and knew if he hit us, we were both dead! I had no choice but to sit still and wait for the deadly impact or drive into oncoming traffic! I found myself saying, "Help me, Jesus," and at that split second, I felt something very strong push my car sideways, out of the way, and the SUV zoomed by. I was stunned and filled with relief and amazement! I knew it was God or an Angel. Jesus heard my prayer! I witnessed God's miracle in plain sight on that day and have never seen anything like it before.

I watched as the speeding vehicle hit the ditch, flipped up in the air into a complete 360 side flip, then landed on its tires on the opposite side of the ditch. It was terrifying! I drove my car off the highway, grabbed my baby son, and jumped out of my car. I held that baby closer than ever before and thanked God.

The SUV driver jumped out of his vehicle in complete astonishment and ran to me, asking if I was ok. I said yes, still shaking, and asked him if he was ok. He said he was fine and didn't notice a scratch or a dent on either vehicle.

Another man ran to the scene with his eyes wide open in astonishment and said, "I saw the whole thing from the roof of my house." He shook his head as if he couldn't believe what he had just witnessed.

To this very day, I thank God for saving my son's life as well as mine. I truly witnessed a miracle.

"The Lord is my rock and my fortress and my deliverer; My God, my strength, in whom I will trust; My shield and the horn of my salvation, my stronghold" (Psalms 18:2 NKJV).

"Look to Me, and be saved, All you ends of the earth! For I am God, and there is no other" (Isaiah 45:22 NKJV).

"In the name of our Lord Jesus Christ, when you are gathered together, along with my spirit, with the power of our Lord Jesus Christ ..." (1 Corinthians 5:4 NKJV).

Diana Baum lives in Northern New Mexico with her husband and children.

Chapter 7

It Was God All Along!

By Tina

Many times, when I was in the deep dark abyss of my addiction and homelessness, I could hear Him talking to me. Whispers in my ear, like a distant voice. But I wouldn't listen enough. I knew it was God, but I wasn't ready to embrace it. I would hear Him every time I was in a really terrible place.

When I lost everything—my family, my kids, trust, my humanity—He called out to me, "There is a better way."

When I was a part of or a witness to unspeakable acts, He whispered, "Come into the light." I did not listen.

When I awoke from my third overdose, He said to me, "It is not your time."

When I stopped three seconds short of killing a man, He said to me, "You are not a murderer." So, I stopped and didn't kill him, but I still didn't listen deep enough.

A friend of mine (who was what we called on the streets "an innocent" because he wasn't involved in the terrible, immoral things around him; he just happened to be homeless and kept to himself) was in the wrong place at the wrong time. He got rolled up in the area rug and lit on fire in an alley. I wasn't there when it happened, but I wasn't far away, so I heard about it while the rug was still burning. I was filled with a pain that is difficult to describe—shock, deep sadness, and fear for my own life. Could I be next? While trying to process this horror, I heard Him say, "Turn to me."

Every time I heard the whispers, I knew it was God. I don't know how I knew; I just believed it, and each time I heard His words, I felt very comforted. But I was never ready to do anything about it until....

.... Almost two years later, sitting in jail, as I had done so many times before, I heard Him say, "I will sit with you." At that moment, I was ready to listen. I was ready to turn to God! I found myself finally able to break free from the life I was in. I was ready to listen to and heed His words.

God gave me the courage and strength to break my bonds of addiction. I was FREE to walk out of the darkness and into the light. I fell to my knees and lifted my face to the sky. I said to Him, "Thank you, thank you for always being with me when I needed you most; I love you."

My husband was released from prison, and we were reunited. At the time, we were sleeping in someone's car, and the owner didn't know. We had to sneak into it after dark and leave before the sun came up so no one would catch us. One day, I took my husband's hand and said, "It's time." We soon got an apartment, and then we got furniture. I got new glasses and fixed my teeth. The darkness was finally behind us. The best part of all is we got our kids back! A year later, we rented an RV and went on our first vacation! I wouldn't give this up for anything!

I think back on all those times I heard God talking to me, asking me to go towards him when all those horrible things were happening. Had I paid more attention then, I know I would have gotten out of my situation sooner.

Fear not, for I am with you; Be not dismayed, for I am your God. I will strengthen you, Yes, I will help you, I will uphold you with My righteous right hand (Isaiah 41:10).

Since October 1, 2017, I have been free from drugs. My faith and my love for God are stronger than ever. I don't hear Him as much these days, but I know He is still with me every step I take.

I can do all things through Christ who strengthens me (Philippians 4:13).

Tina is a Peer Recovery Navigator for COPA Health

Chapter 8

We Gave Despite Trying Times & God's Goodness Shined Upon Us

By Larry Socea

My wife, Maggi, and I were "Born Again" in 1980. Immediately after deciding to trust Christ for our salvation, we committed to regular church attendance, daily study of the scriptures, and frequent volunteering in various ministries in the church. We also began donating what we thought was a "reasonable" amount to church and other Christian ministries. Although the amount was nowhere near what could be considered a tithe, it was certainly more than we had ever given to charity.

Fast forward to the fall of 1997, seventeen years later. We were still giving a reasonable amount when our pastor preached a 4-part series on the "Power of Tithing." We were moved by the content of the messages and the obvious scriptural support he presented. So, at the end of the series, in early November, we began to faithfully tithe a true 10% of our income to the church.

That worked well until, just 6 weeks into our commitment, I was laid off from my Job. That was hardly an expected outcome of our obedience in committing to tithe. Regardless, my separation package included two months of income to give me time to find another job. So, we decided that, even though I felt pressured to conserve as much money as possible until I found work, we would continue to tithe as if I was still employed since I would receive pay commensurate with that scenario. We reasoned that we would cut back on our giving if I did not have work at the end of the two months.

On the final Sunday of the two months of separation pay, I still did not have a job or any prospects for employment. Despite that, we tithed that day. The next morning, "out of the blue," I received a call from a previous employer with whom I had had no contact for almost two years. Their office manager emailed a resignation letter to them over the weekend. They asked if I could cover the office for two weeks until they hired a replacement. Of course, I said, "Yes!" And so, we tithed for two more weeks. At the end of the initial two weeks, they had not yet found a suitable candidate, so they contracted me for two more weeks. And we tithed those two weeks as well. Then another two-week extension allowed us to continue tithing. When the six weeks were complete, they finally hired a new office manager, and I was again "unemployed."

The following week, a contact at church asked if I could

consult with their company on a small business project. I could. And I did. For two weeks. Continuing through a series of Divinely appointed "coincidences," I remained temporarily employed for 18 months, never during the entire period having a commitment from any employer for more than two weeks of scheduled work. And never missing a single week's tithe!

At the end of the 18 months, I finally landed a long-term contract that turned into four years of very profitable work, allowing us to continue to tithe and generously go beyond.

The lessons we learned from this were ....

- We do not have to fear responding to our heart-felt call from God.
- He who calls is faithful to provide everything we need to respond to His call
- The anticipated path of obedience may vary significantly from the actual path we experience
- Though God honors those who answer, it is not necessarily easy for us to fulfill the call.

And all the tithe of the land, whether of the seed of the land, or of the fruit of the tree, is the LORD'S: it is holy unto the LORD (Lev 27:30).

And concerning the tithe of the herd, or of the flock, even of whatsoever passeth under the rod, the tenth

shall be holy unto the LORD (Leviticus 27:32).

Then there shall be a place which the LORD your God shall choose to cause his name to dwell there; thither shall ye bring all that I command you; your burnt offerings, and your sacrifices, your tithes, and the heave offering of your hand, and all your choice vows which ye vow unto the LORD (Deuteronomy 12:11).

Larry Socea is the Associate Pastor
at Ascent Bible Church, Santa Fe, New Mexico
larry.socea@ascentbible.church
Mobile: 714-369-7676

Chapter 9

Fun Getaway Turns Into a Life Calling

By Roberta Carter

My life before my calling was self-centered and pride-filled, especially in my first marriage. I thought the answers to problems were up to me to fix, so I always tried to force things to make them better. I was also a people pleaser who wanted to make sure that others liked me. As a child, I always sought ways to please my parents and never disappoint them. As an adult, this attribute was magnified as my circle of friends increased. My priorities were always my children, husband, family, and others.

I was the one with the answers, who had to fix everything in marriage. That's what I did in my 1st marriage. I didn't want to make the same mistakes twice.

God's calling for me was to marriage ministry, which I never imagined. It began when my husband and I were given a complimentary gift certificate to a marriage conference several years ago. It was a gift offered after church services one day. That told me we were meant to have it. My heart leaped with joy as we received our gift. It would be a relaxing, fun getaway with my husband. I was in my 2nd marriage, and we had already taken the first step toward a successful marriage: God was the center of our marriage. Our marriage was focused on Jesus Christ and the people around us. This conference was an opening for us to learn how to continue on the right path together. I was open to learning and determined not to make the same mistakes I made in my 1st marriage. I knew our marriage had a mission because of a study I had participated in called "Marriage on a Mission," but I wasn't sure what this meant at the time. I knew that my husband and I needed practical everyday tools to facilitate our daily challenges, such as enhancing our communication skills, encouraging positive blended-family interactions, making wise financial decisions, and motivation to continually thrive. So, I was looking forward to this opportunity, never imagining that my life was about to transform.

We listened and took notes throughout the conference. The presenting couples shared God's purpose for our marriage: God created marriage for oneness with Him and each other. Because of the fall of Adam and Eve in the Garden of Eden, our oneness with God and each other is broken. God sent Jesus to restore our oneness. God restores oneness as we accept Jesus as our Savior. My new life with Jesus and oneness with my spouse impact others.

The rapid beating of my heart expressed my excitement

about sharing this with others. For the first time, I knew my husband wasn't my enemy. I always felt judged, as if we were in an antagonistic pattern with each other, and I didn't know how to break it. I realized God gave me my husband as a gift; we are meant to cherish and love each other. This conference was a life-changing event for me.

> **Wives, submit yourselves unto your own husbands, as unto the Lord. For the husband is the head of the wife, even as Christ is the head of the church: as he is the savior of the body. Therefore, as the church is subject unto Christ, so let the wives be to their own husbands in everything. Husbands, love your wives, even as Christ also loved the church, and gave himself for it, that he might sanctify and cleanse it with the washing of the word, that he might present to himself a glorious church, not having spot, or wrinkle, or any such thing: but that it should be holy and without blemish. So ought men to love their wives as their own bodies. He that loveth his wife loveth himself (Ephesians 5:22-28).**

On the last day of the conference, we were asked to complete a questionnaire. I clearly heard the Holy Spirit open my heart to helping other couples in their marriages. This surprised me! I asked God how He could use me, a divorcee in a second marriage, to help other couples? When I first got divorced, I felt like I had a big "D" on my forehead. We had been seen as the happy couple with the perfect life. It was embarrassing, and I carried that guilt with me for a long time. It was a huge *ah-ha* moment when I realized God had forgiven my sins, and I didn't need to look back anymore. After attending, I heard God say to me, "Remember Roberta, I'm going to use you, and I will equip you. And you can use the story of your first marriage and divorce to help others. I will use the foolish things of this world to confound the wise."

I looked forward to following God's calling on my life. I followed God's calling obediently and lovingly. I knew that this was part of His plan for my life. The mission for my marriage was revealed, and I took it very seriously.

My next step was to volunteer with our local marriage conference team. Several times, I met with the team for training, encouragement, support, and prayer. God lovingly directed me with my roles and responsibilities in the ministry. The following year, after my first conference, I served with the logistics team, helping with registration.

After attending the conference, I knew that I had to be intentional with my time, meals, hobbies, and times of rest by not just leaving with the tools I learned but also using them. The mission God gave me was to share the gospel of hope and bear fruit. I began looking at the needs around me and felt inspired to help. Instead of praying for couples' marriages in general, we started praying for specific couples. God gave me new life so that I could, through His strength, give to others.

I am the vine, ye are the branches, He that abideth in me, and I in him, the same brighten forth much fruit: for without me ye can do nothing (John 15:5).

I must stay rooted in Him to bear fruit. Being on mission required intentionally finding ways to invest my time to demonstrate love and Christ's grace to others. The group marriage Bible studies, one-on-one prayer time with couples, and group meetings to pray for couples attending marriage conferences were all part of the ministry.

To help build strong marriages, God is transforming me into His image and likeness. God wants me to be around other people, interacting and thriving together. Next, bearing fruit involved introducing others to Christ and helping them grow in their faith. I began to share the gift of hospitality with others, sharing meals together and taking time to listen. It was a way to express God's love and show how Jesus changes lives and redeems our past, present, and future.

My life changed after I followed God's instructions. Instead of focusing only on my marriage, I prayed for other marriages. I asked God for opportunities to help couples whose marriages were in challenging situations. I told others about transformational changes at the marriage conferences and Bible studies. In addition, if couples needed more assistance, God directed couples to Biblical marriage counseling.

This experience of receiving and following this calling

has strengthened my faith, but it hasn't always been easy. God has shown me that in my weakness, He is strong. One year, I attended a marriage conference on my own, which was very difficult. My husband couldn't attend due to a debilitating illness. This caused a division in our marriage whereby my trust was challenged. I had to go before the Lord and ask Him, "How can I trust him again?" I knew it was time to trust God and not my feelings. And at the same time, COVID hit, and we all went on lockdown, which meant my husband and I were isolated. What I thought would be the worst of times turned into a blessing. I kept my eyes on the Lord, and instead of stepping back, I stepped into our marriage encouraged. We worked together. That's what marriage is. The difficult situation separated us, but God brought us back to oneness from a place where we had drifted. God taught me patience and showed me how to move forward. I heard God say, "Just give it time and continue in forgiveness. You need to forgive, and I will do what needs to be done with him." This took me a full year, but I gave him the benefit of the doubt, and God started changing both of our hearts.

From the beginning of this challenge, God showed me that I needed to attend the conference to help others and be a light in the darkness. I was hesitant. I didn't want questions since I was there alone. But I followed God's guidance, despite myself. Many people asked me about my husband,

and I had to humble myself before others and receive their love and support. I wanted no questions, but God wanted me to be receptive to receiving, which was the opposite of what I was used to. As a result, I got much love, encouragement, and prayer for us both. I left feeling very, very loved and supported. But mostly, I thanked my Lord for bringing me there. It allowed me to help others, which I knew was all for His glory and honor. God wants to see marriages work. This was for God. Now, I can pray for those who are in similar situations. God has assured me that He has created marriages for oneness with Him and each other.

And the Lord God said, It is not good that the man should be alone; I will make a help meet for him (Genesis 2:18).

God continues to open doors for us. We are still helping others in their marriage, more than ever. Not only are we guiding couples, but we are teaching them to turn around and help others. This is indeed a calling. God is bringing others into my life that need help. It's a holy covenant and an honor.

My advice to help you recognize God's calling is to pray. God asks us to pray without ceasing. In the quiet moments of your day, seek His perfect will for your life. He already knows the desires of our hearts, and He will give us what we need. Additionally, God will speak to you through other people. Often, God will confirm your specific calling through another person. Read your Bible daily to receive God's instructions in righteousness. He will direct your steps. His Word is a Light unto our path. God sometimes places us in unique circumstances outside of our comfort zone. God's ways are not our ways. Be open to His calling in your life, and your life will be transformed.

Roberta Carter is a retired teacher
505-920-7204 carter.roberta1@gmail.com
The marriage ministry Roberta was called to is:
Family Life Weekend to Remember
TimSteele@FamilyLife.com

Chapter 10

Angry at the World YET God Heard My Plea, Anyway!

By Donna Nelson Castelonia

In July of 2012, I began the journey of surrender and being transformed by God that continues to amaze and humble me.

At 50 years old, I found myself living in my aunt's basement, suicidal and addicted to alcohol. I had been divorced for the 2nd time at forty years old, and a few years later, with my two children in college, I was forced to sell my home and declare bankruptcy. I was wrapped up in self-pity, shame, resentment, and remorse and drank more and more to numb the pain and face the mess of a life I was living. I was angry at the world and financially, spiritually, mentally, and emotionally empty. I believed if there WAS a God, I certainly didn't like him, and he certainly didn't like me based on all the "bad" things that happened in my life. Every day I woke up was another day I dreaded having to get through. How dark it is before the dawn!

I was agnostic up to that point in my life. I definitely did not spend any time in prayer, meditation, church, or scripture. Unknowingly, I was living a life full of false pride and lacked the humility to ask for help. My identity was in things of the world, and I grabbed onto everything I could to feel like I had worth and value. I used my appearance, career, husbands, children, talents, and personality. I looked to people for approval and love and to make me feel secure and safe and a sense of belonging. I knew nothing of God's love and teachings nor his mercy and grace.

All that changed on July 4th, 2012, when I finally opened my heart to listen to a Christian minister at my best friend's birthday party. I had met him six months earlier when he stopped me in the middle of a conversation. He shared with me that he didn't know what I was going through, but God just spoke to him, and he wanted me to know that I'm loved and everything is going to be okay. The tears immediately flowed, followed by anger at him for opening wounds I was so desperately trying to drink away. We saw him a few more times after that, where he tried talking with me, and I tried avoiding conversation with the "Jesus Freak."

But on that particular day at that birthday party, God graced me with an open mind and a willing heart. I listened to what he told me about God's love, forgiveness, and mercy. He suggested I ask this God into my heart and let him heal me. He advised that I just talk to him, which is praying, and sit in stillness to listen, which is meditating.

Later that night, I got on my knees for the first time and prayed these words: "God, I don't know who you are or what you are or IF you are, but I want to know you. Please come into my heart and show me the truth of who you are and who I am, and help me." And then I just stayed there on my knees in stillness. After a few minutes, I was overcome with an indescribable feeling of peace. I was flooded with a love I had never felt before, along with goosebumps and tingling. I began to weep and realized that maybe all these people with a relationship with God were not "freaks" after all.

And ye shall seek Me and find Me, when ye shall search for Me with all your heart (Jeremiah 29:13).

I had no idea how much my life would change starting with that night! I continued to get on my knees almost daily, asking God to help me with my mess of a life. Then I would sit in stillness, wanting to feel that incredible feeling again. It was during those moments I first heard God's calling. The thought would drop into my head, "You're an alcoholic; you need AA," when I prayed. I didn't listen and continued to drink despite trying so hard not to.

On the week of my 50th birthday in August, I was arrested for drunk driving and lost my license for six months. I wrestled with my human thoughts that told me God WASN'T helping me at all. And I wrestled with God's

92

calling that told me to go to AA. Everything I used to get a sense of SELF was stripped away, and that's what I needed to let God in. My kids were grown and gone, so I felt my identity and worth as a mother were over. I was no longer a wife, a homeowner, a dog owner, a car owner, or even someone who could DRIVE! I was barely working, so I didn't feel any sense of identity from that either. I was terrified to admit to myself and others that I really WAS addicted to alcohol. It took me another six months before I finally went to my first AA meeting in January 2013. I felt God's presence in that meeting, and once again, a profound thought dropped into my head, saying, "Everything will be ok now; you're where you're supposed to be." I felt hope for the first time in years.

I knew nothing of the twelve-step program of AA and its goals to guide us to surrender to God and allow him to be the director of our life, have a spiritual awakening from working the steps, and then be of service to him and his people by helping others get sober. I didn't think I was capable of helping anyone at that point, as I was pretty helpless and useless. Little did I know how much God would transform and use me to help inspire and encourage others.

Several months after continuing to attend meetings, getting a sponsor, and working the steps, I had a profound vision. It was November, and I was in bed reading a book titled "The World's Greatest Salesman" by Og Mandino. I put the book down to go to sleep. As I lay in bed, I saw an impulse sprinkler watering a lawn, one of those that goes around in circles, making a *choot-choot-choot* sound. I literally heard the sound. It was November, so no one was watering their lawn. It wouldn't leave my mind, so I sat up to meditate on what it meant. God showed me that I was the sprinkler, the grass was people, the water was words coming from my mouth that would help them grow, and the part that shuts off the water supply to make it move was my hand covering my mouth. He called me to start speaking and sharing my experiences and what I was learning from AA, Bible study, readings, meditation classes, etc. Until then, I rarely shared in AA meetings, as I felt unqualified. I hadn't realized that it was HIM using me as a channel and speaking through me to help others. I started raising my hand and sharing at meetings and going on speaking commitments for AA. Soon after, women started asking me to sponsor them and take them through the twelve steps. God was using my words to help people grow. ME! Simply Amazing!

I've grown to recognize how my dark times became a testimony and an encouragement to help others out of their dark times. And I'm deeply blessed every time I mentor other women and watch their light come on.

I believe God talks to us in all kinds of ways. Sometimes,

it's through prayer and meditation, sometimes through other people, and sometimes through readings or "coincidences." It's up to me to pay attention, hear the calling, and take action. And it's not always easy.

In early 2014, I was praying for career guidance. I was no longer feeling any enjoyment or passion as a realtor and wanted to go to work "for God." My mind saw that as a ministry, but God had other plans. One day shortly after I prayed, I received a call from a realtor and caught myself asking him if he needed a buyer's agent, as I was looking for a change. He said he couldn't believe I had just asked that, as his partner and he had a meeting that morning that they needed to hire one. They were both Christians and starting a team. They now own two real estate offices. I have been on their team for seven years in a culture and leadership where I'm thriving and prospering and teaching and helping other agents and those I help in AA. God knew exactly where to place me to be served and be of service to him.

Today, I do my best to surrender daily to God's guidance, and my life just seems to flourish. I've remained sober since 2013. I've since remarried and purchased a lakefront home on Lake Hopatcong, NJ. The trials and tribulations still come, but they lead to more growth, which God uses to help others through the same struggles. I started teaching meditation classes to help people tap into that inner guidance system that has transformed me and my life. I firmly believe that God comes to those who seek him. May this story bless and encourage you.

And He said unto me, "My grace is sufficient for thee: for my strength is made perfect in weakness (2 Corinthians 12:9).

❦❦❦

Donna Nelson Castelonia lives in NJ
Real Estate: DonnaNelson@kw.com.
Meditation classes or addiction issues:
Growthwithdonna@gmail.com

Chapter 11

Nothing Specific; I Just Know!

By Glenn Crooker

I thought I was going to write about some profound inspirational experience, but instead, I'd like to share that for me, it's about simply knowing God has ALWAYS been with me through the good and bad, happy and sad. Every moment, he's been there and never left me.

What I do every day is by his guidance. Over time, the bad I did turned into the good I do, EVERY DAY. That is God.

I am where I am, doing what I do EVERY DAY because of him.

I thank HIM for never leaving me."

For we walk by faith, not by sight (2 Corinthians 5:7 NKJV).

But let him ask in faith, with no doubting, for he who doubts is like a wave of the sea driven and tossed by the wind (James 1:6 NKJV).

Glenn E. Crooker is a Case Manager for Behavioral Health at COPA Health, Phoenix, Arizona

Chapter 12

Looking Back Realizing that I am Guided

By Liza Davis

- My Date with Destiny: God Can Be Romantic
- God Sent Me Three Messengers
- How Do I Follow God's Guidance Now?

My Date with Destiny: God Can Be Romantic

During meditation, I realized that all I truly wanted was an amazing, loving husband and two beautiful children. I envisioned paradise: a beautiful garden with me and my future husband and the kids playing around and laughing.

Inspired by that vision, I decided to take massive action to go and find that man or be found by him. So, on one beautiful December day, I made myself comfortable at a cozy downtown Los Angeles Starbucks and created a description of my future husband. When I was done, my dream man and everything I ever wanted to find in a husband were right there in front of my eyes. He was staring at me from my computer screen. The love of my life was neatly organized into 109 musts, wants, and nice-to-haves characteristics. This man was simply amazing; we were completely in love with each other; he wanted to marry me and have children together. The interesting part was that when I finished and looked at what I had created, I really felt that I was in love with this man already. I was in love with him before I ever met him.

For the next few months, I found myself really busy going on dates with different people and enjoying great—or sometimes not as great—conversations. It was a bit scary and awkward at first, but then it turned out to be fun, and I was excited to meet my husband.

I also said this special prayer to open myself up to love. I repeated to myself, "God, come onto my heart; I am open to you. Love, come into my heart; I am open to you." I repeated this over and over again, and I felt more open. I felt a shift.

But my God shall supply all your need according to His riches in glory by Christ Jesus (Philippians 4:19).

The First Date: One day, I went out on a date to meet with Paul. We met at the beautiful beach in Palos Verdes, California. He greeted me with a lovely red rose and a magnetic smile. We took a pleasant walk along the shore and then had a delightful lunch by the ocean's edge. I considered two dishes, and he ordered both of them for us to share. I loved the way he looked at me and the way he really listened. I loved how he talked, how he walked, how he looked, how he later would take my hand, how he greeted the sunset, and the quiet confidence he exuded. His whole presence made me feel bliss.

The interesting thing was that the beach where I met Paul was the exact same beach where I had been inspired just three months earlier to move to California. Back then, I lived in New York and flew in for the "Date with Destiny" event with Tony Robbins and to visit a friend in LA. She brought me to this very same beach, and I was sitting on those same rocks, walking on that same sand, and looking at that same ocean. This beach was magnetizing me with its beauty and calling me to move to the West Coast. I remember an overpowering feeling in my heart and whole body that it was the right thing to do. A month later, I packed up my world in New York and followed that feeling by moving to California.

As Paul and I sat on that same beach, enjoying each other's company over a wonderful lunch, I experienced that same overpowering feeling of rightness and bliss. Could it really be that God pulled me to this beach all the way from NY to meet my Date with Destiny?

God, Please Give me a Car! When I moved to California three months before meeting Paul, I packed up just a few belongings and left everything else behind. I lived the

California dream and stayed on a mattress at my friend's home. While I truly wanted a husband and two children, I still needed a job, new business income— or some kind of income—a home, a car, and a dog would be nice, too. That's about it.

The car was actually at the top of that list. While living in NY, being car-less was the way to go, but I really needed a car in LA! After plenty of research, I decided to get a red Mazda. I went to a nearby dealership, and there it was—my beautiful red Mazda... I really liked it. As I visualized how great I would look driving in that gorgeous car to all my business meetings and dates, I got some distressing news. Apparently, my proof of income— or lack thereof at the time—wasn't sufficient to buy that vehicle or any other kind of vehicle.

After five more unsettling and unsuccessful visits to different dealerships, I sat and thought, "Wow, this is really hard. No one wants to give me a car, and the money is running out, and I don't even know how I am going to pay for things." I was sitting and crying and wondering what to do. I knew that I needed to shift my thoughts. I meditated, visualized, and convinced myself that God would somehow help me get a car. It didn't matter what they told me. Somehow, I was going to get that car. After a while, I started crying again, but I was no longer feeling sorry for myself. Instead, I was feeling a powerful release, knowing that it was going to happen...somehow.

The young lions lack and suffer hunger; But those who seek the Lord shall not lack any good thing (Psalms 34:10).

I stopped going to dealerships for a while. I was visualizing every day that I would get my perfect car and my perfect husband. I was asking God to help me and feeling grateful for this amazing future.

After I met Paul and we started dating, I was shocked to discover that he just happened to have an extra car—a red Mazda! The EXACT same car I wanted but couldn't get. Eventually, he gave me that car—no down payment, no credit check, and no monthly payments necessary. What were the odds of me falling in love with this amazing man who just so happened to have a red Mazda—an extra one? It was a true blessing!

The Greatest Gift: When I finally shared with Paul that list of 109 traits my husband would have, he said, "I did pretty well!" He got 108 out of 109 things because he didn't like to dance. Paul then said dancing was a stretch goal and signed up for a dancing class to dance with me at our wedding.

In 2022, we celebrated our tenth anniversary. It has been the happiest time of our lives. We have four beautiful children (we were blessed with more than I could imagine). The miracle red Mazda grew with the family and evolved into a larger model to fit the entire clan, including our beautiful dog. We are truly blessed. Paul is my dream come true. I love how he says the purpose of his life is to always keep me happy and fulfilled. He is certainly living that purpose.

I once got a question at a Toastmasters public speaking meeting: "What is the best gift you have ever gotten?" For me, it's Paul. He is the greatest gift from God and the best thing that ever happened to me. And it all started with a deep desire to meet my husband and the feeling that I needed to move to California. God took care of me in ways that were beyond my dreams!

And now abide faith, hope and love, these three; but the greatest of these is love (1 Corinthians 13:13 NKJV).

God Sent Me Three Messengers

It's been twelve years since I met my husband. As I fulfilled my deep desire to be happily married and have children, some new passions opened up for me.

For several years, I have felt a calling for natural healing and a healthy lifestyle. It all started with the birth of my first child, when my labor lasted for one week (as in seven days!). I wanted to have this peaceful natural birthing experience with hypnobirthing. It ended up being the most complicated and LONG process, ending with lots of inter-ventions, a C-section, and quite a few complications. I kept trying to figure out, *why did it happen?* That was one of the things that led me to learn about natural healing in search of the answers. Later, as one of my sons and my husband had some medical challenges, I became even more obsessed with this topic.

I spent hours and hours reading books on the topic, re-searching holistic ways, and practicing it primarily with my family and friends. I have seen incredible results with peo-ple naturally lowering high blood pressure, improving cho-lesterol, curing acid reflux, relieving anxiety, losing weight, and switching to a healthier lifestyle. If someone has a head-ache, back pain, or any medical condition, I go on a mission to go and find natural ways to help this person. As a re-sult, my family now has quite a healthy lifestyle, despite the kids' complaints; they'd rather be eating candy!

Professionally, I have been primarily doing dating, ca-reer, and executive coaching for over ten years. While do-ing a modest amount of health coaching with some of my clients, I wanted to do it more. Much more. I yearned to take health coaching and healing to a much higher level and really help many people.

At the same time, something was holding me back. I had these thoughts going through my mind: *How am I going to do that? Am I good enough? I am not a doctor. I don't have enough credentials for it. Why should people listen to me? What happens if I can't help some people? Many of my views are untraditional compared to modern Western medicine; what are people going to think? There are so many ways and techniques of helping people to heal; how do I combine them all, or which one do I use? I don't know where to start.*

This internal struggle was brewing in my mind for a couple of years until I volunteered at a Tony Robbins event one day. During this event, we underwent a process of changing limiting beliefs, and I decided to work on my beliefs around healing and health coaching.

I was able to release my old beliefs: *I don't know where to start. I don't have the credentials. I am not good enough.* Here are the new beliefs that came to me as I closed my eyes and surrendered to God:

I am a healer.
I am guided.
The people who are supposed to help me
will come into my life.
The people that I am supposed to help
will come into my life.

I was repeating those new beliefs out loud over and over again. I said it with emotion; I said it with passion; I said it like I believed it. At first, I had resistance in my body; I felt tension in my forehead. I was very tentative even sharing those words with other participants. Saying, "I am a healer," seemed weird and uncomfortable. Yet, I kept saying those words repeatedly, and after a while, I felt a bit more at ease with it. As I went home that night, I wondered if this stuff was actually going to work. Did I really change my beliefs, or was it just a nice exercise?

The Next Day: The next morning, as thousands of people from all over the world were gathering by the convention center to see Tony Robbins, I was sent to greet participants at the opposite side of the venue from where I usually worked. When the convention center doors finally opened, the crowds rushed through and raced to get the best seats. The entryway quickly emptied out, and I was enjoying a gorgeous warm November day in West Palm Beach.

Then suddenly, this man said, "Blessed." He came to me and asked me, "Have I met you at a Joe Dispenza event?" I was astounded by this question. I learned a lot about healing and health from Joe Dispenza and always wanted to attend one of his events, but it seemed too complicated.

This nice man, Jeff, was telling me how he went to different countries and exotic islands to see the events. I asked him, "How long is the seminar?" He said, "Seven days." The cost was a few thousand dollars, too. I listened to this and thought, *Wow, my husband would just love for me to go to some island for a week and spend a few thousand dollars while he is staying at home and watching our four kids!*

CHAPTER 12

When I asked where the events would be, Jeff said Gay-lord Texan Hotel in Grapevine, Texas, but it was not being advertised yet. My eyes widened as this hotel "happened to be" 15 MINUTES away from my house! This man did not even know where I lived!

This stranger approached me on the street to let me know there was a training (not yet advertised) by my number-one healing teacher fifteen minutes away from my house? I had complete confidence that God sent Jeff to me as a messenger to help me find direction!

Where do I start with health coaching and healing? Who do I follow? I now had the answers. My husband and I are now going to that Joe Dispenza event. I know that this is exactly where I am supposed to be.

My encounters didn't end there. That same day I also ran into an old friend who had been doing health coaching for over twenty years. He told me how I could use what I already knew to do Health Coaching right there and then and broke down everything I needed to do to get started.

It also turned out that this very day a famous healer just happened to be making a special presentation for Tony's volunteers. I was sitting in the first row and listening to all the advice on how one can help heal people.

I felt so guided. People who were supposed to help me were coming into my life.

I will instruct you and teach you in the way you

107

should go; I will guide you with My eye (Psalms 32:8 NKJV).

They came quickly: three messengers the very next day with three important messages:

- Healing can be learned.
- I already have a lot of what I need.
- I AM a healer, and this is the right path.

All I need to do is trust that God is guiding me and follow his guidance. These messages gave me a clear plan of how I would start, what I would learn, and what I could do right then.

By the way, I really helped some people that day who came straight to me. I felt they were also sent to me because I had a special message for them.

Eight Months Later: I have been working with individuals and groups of people, helping them in both emotional and physical healing. I am also on my way to learning more advanced techniques and powerful healing tools. I am grateful to God for guiding me and sending me the answers the next day.

After these experiences, I often remind myself that I am guided whenever I have a challenge or an unanswered question, and the answers come to me one way or another.

Call to Me and I will answer you, and show you

great and mighty things, which you do not know (Jeremiah 33:3 NKJV).

How Do I Follow God's Guidance Now?

When I was volunteering at Tony Robbins' event, "Date with Destiny," we went through a process of changing our primary question. That is the question people ask themselves every day, often many times a day, that defines the quality of their lives. I decided to upgrade my old question and make my new question, "How do I follow God's guidance now?"

The next day after I changed my question, I wanted to make myself more comfortable enjoying the virtual event. I needed to move my office chair from one room to another. It's a BIG chair, and the doorway is quite narrow. I pushed the chair through one way, then another, sideways, the other side, upside down, nothing!

I thought, *my husband got it in there, so it has to come out somehow!* Then I tried again, squeezing it through any other way I could imagine. After ten minutes, I was getting quite frustrated and ready to quit and ask my husband to get it out, as he is really good with this stuff.

Then I thought, *Hold on, what's my new primary question? How do I follow God's guidance now?* Well, I HAVE TO HAVE SOME GUIDANCE FIRST! Then I closed my eyes and surrendered to receiving that "get the chair through the door" guidance. An image came into my mind to have the wheels out first. I followed it and wiggled it for a minute, and it came out!

Later that day, my husband saw me sitting in that chair in another room and asked me, "How did you get this chair out of that room?" Of course, I shared the story with him. He said, "Wow, that's impressive; I had to disassemble it to get it in there!"

Months have passed, and my husband still doesn't know how to get the chair out of that room, and he is still impressed. When I think that I am unsure how to do something or plainly think, "I don't know," I remind myself that "I am guided." I then surrender, ask what I want to know, and meditate on it. God usually sends the answer, and it's often right away. Sometimes, other people come into my life to answer that question.

Convert your "I don't know's" into "I am guided," and trust that you will get an answer.

Ask, and it will be given to you; seek, and you will find; knock, and it will be opened to you. For everyone who asks receives, and he who seeks finds and to him who knocks it will be opened (Matthew 7: 7-8 NKJV).

I now know that I am guided. As I look back at those experiences in my life and many more, I am convinced of that. I am learning to consciously turn to God's guidance in my life more and more. Whether it's a big decision or a small thing, just closing my eyes, clearing my thoughts, and trusting that I will get guidance usually brings me further than trying to work something out in my head for hours, days, or months. It makes life easier, melts stress, and gets much better solutions. I intend to let go and let God much more in my life and tap into this greater power far beyond my understanding.

Trust in the Lord with all your heart, and lean not on your own understanding; In all your ways acknowledge Him and He shall direct your paths (Proverbs 3: 5-6 NKJV).

Liza Davis specializes in helping women find their ideal relationship. She is a co-author of *Love and Coaching with John Gray*, (author of Men are from Mars, Women are from Venus) and a previous owner of Mars Venus Coaching & Training. Liza has worked with the finest coaching organizations in the world. She is happily married to the man of her dreams and has four children. To learn more about Liza, go to www.CoachingAndTraining.com

Chapter 13

God Called Us To Guatemala

By Phillip and Dianna

We began as short-term foster parents. These children would come into our home while their parents awaited a court hearing. Some of the children came into our home with other siblings, others alone. All children were scared and crying. Our job was to comfort them, give them safety, and assure them all would be okay. We, at times, would stay awake all night, listening to their cries. It was always bittersweet when the social worker called to say, "We have found a permanent foster family." By this time, we had already bonded with the children, and it was very hard to say goodbye. All we could do was put them in our heart safe. We had grown to love these children, and they would NEVER be forgotten. Our prayers would go with them. We had twenty-eight children over eighteen years.

God Was Watching Us: One quiet afternoon, we received a surprise phone call. "Hello, my name is Cindy. I am the director of an orphanage in Guatemala. Is this Dianna and Phillip?" She continued to tell me how our name came up several times in conversation with some of her Christian friends. Cindy needed house parents at the Orphanage and offered us the role, hoping we would accept. Cindy ended the conversation with, "I will call in a week or so. I ask you to pray about it."

WHAT?! We did not even know where Guatemala was!!!! This was before we had the internet, so we brought out our encyclopedia to look it up and start figuring things out. We counseled with our pastor, prayed, and asked God what to do. We soon got a letter and pictures of the girls we would take care of. Our hearts began to melt as we learned their names and prayed for them.

Road Trip! We chose to drive to Guatemala. What were we thinking?! It was about 2000 miles away and would take at least thirty-five hours to drive, plus stopping for rest and food. And there was no Google Maps!

When we arrived in Guatemala City, Guatemala, we stopped to look at the map. It was gone! We lost it! We had no idea which way to go. This was before cell phones. We decided to just drive and trust God to get us there! So, we headed out of the city. We asked along the way which way to Antigua. Once in Antigua, with no map, we began to ask God, "Lord, show us the way; sorry we lost the map." We wondered if it was too much to ask God to lead us to the orphanage!

We came to a T-intersection. Right or left? We had no idea. A man on a bicycle stopped next to us. We asked, "We need to go to Principe de Paz Orphanage; would you know where it is?"

"Yes!" he says.

We followed this friendly man to the gate of the orphanage.

God knew we would ask; he sent a man to show us the way. God wanted us there. We were one day late, but we made it!

Thy word is a lamp unto my feet, and a light unto my path (Psalm 119: 105).

Cause me to know the way wherein I should walk: For I lift up my soul unto thee (Psalm 143:8).

On day two, we began our work. We knew these girls already. They were the ones we prayed for and fell in love with them.

Work was hard. Twenty-four girls, all ages. The youngest, three years old. When one became sick with the mumps, all did. We were Mom and Dad to them. Our term ended one year later. They are in our hearts forevermore. Yes, we are still praying for all of them by name. We shall see them again with our Lord when the time comes for all of us to be together again.

We will always remember how God surprised us with this task of caring for his needy children. It was an honor to serve. We will also remember how God made sure we got there.

Who needs a map?!

Phillip and Dianna enjoy living in the beautiful mountains of Northern New Mexico.

Chapter 14

In the End, My Failure Was God Paving My Path

By Anonymous

Someone asked me at a dinner party last weekend, "Are you spiritual?" I said, "yes." He proceeded to share that he and his wife differ in their beliefs. He explained that his wife was a devout Catholic, and he wasn't. He further shared that he considers himself spiritual and asked what I thought about organized religion. Wow…what a question to be asked at a lighthearted dinner party; I was about to take a bite of salad. I was surprised at my quick response. I said to him, "I feel that religion is a human attempt … to define one's spirituality. Whether it be Catholic or another religious belief…I feel we are all just trying to express our spirituality. And, perhaps looking at it through that lens, we can stop analyzing our differences and focus on embracing the spirit of God that we may share."

Okay, so this is supposed to be a story about a calling from God, so why am I sharing a dinner party story? Well, it's because, at that moment, I realized I needed to have the courage to share my story. When asked to write about my experiences regarding "a calling from God," I was very hesitant. I thought to myself, *I have never heard the voice of God, nor have I had a vision of God. How can I write about this topic?* Yet, deep in my heart, I felt I have experienced a "calling," as some say. I decided to put this writing opportunity to the side and just think about it. And I did until this dinner party conversation inspired me to share my experience.

Several years ago, I embarked on a journey to make a career change, as I wanted to work in a profession that held a more meaningful purpose. This was an exciting time, and I felt genuinely intuitive about making this change. I went back to college at fifty years old. I studied science and felt a strong pull in the direction of health care. While taking prerequisite classes, I got a bit sidetracked and chose a specialty area that seemed easy to reach (doable). This path was exciting because I was moving toward a new profession with vast opportunities. With a new career in plain sight, I was moving fast on this road, trying to reach this goal. However, everything started to go wrong on this path, and things didn't feel right. At first, I remember feeling like a square peg trying to fit into a round hole, but I kept persevering. I didn't want to give up. I kept working hard and was motivated mostly by not wanting to fail. Even though I knew in my heart and soul that I had taken a wrong turn, I just refused to give up. I remember thinking each and every day, "I cannot fail."

Then, one after another, roadblocks appeared before me. Big roadblocks! I will name a few. I bumped my head on my car trunk in the college parking lot and had to be taken by ambulance to the hospital. I had a concussion, and they put a dozen surgical staples in the top of my head that night. But I kept going! Shortly after that, I had an accidental chemical exposure in my chemistry class and was ill for many months. Nope...I didn't stop. I couldn't fail! A few months later, I developed a lump in my throat and had a biopsy and treatment. Yes, I finally stopped then. I got off that path abruptly and carried a sense of looming failure for some time, even though I knew I was on the wrong path. Reflecting on those experiences, it seemed like something was trying to get me off that path. Many people around me shared that same observation. Hmm...something to think about.

As time went by, I just waited for clarity. I knew I needed to reconnect with "that feeling," "that pull," "that inspiration from within," and "that calling" to recognize the right path for myself.

During the COVID lockdown, I had the clarity I yearned for. One day, I shared with my child that we all need to do our part to make the world a better place. It sounds a bit cliché, but it was a heartfelt conversation and a teaching moment. We discussed the old saying about *"the pebble in the pond"* as I tried to shift her perspective to a hopeful one during this unsettling time in our world. I asked my child to imagine how just one pebble thrown into a pond creates a ripple effect that, in turn, creates change around it. Positive effects can occur, even with just small acts of kindness. As I heard myself sharing with such passion and faith, I realized I wanted to be *that pebble!* In my own small way, I wanted to positively impact the world by serving those in my community who need support. It was clear at that moment what I needed to do.

The next day I researched universities and, shortly after, applied to my chosen graduate program. I was accepted within a few weeks. It all seemed to happen so fast and with ease. No roadblocks, just an open highway to where I felt I needed to go. I leaped into a master's program with a calm knowing that I was supposed to take this path toward this new profession. I am currently on this journey, and it feels so right! Things are organically happening; my path is unfolding before me. Doors are opening around me, left and right. I feel a sense of belonging and peace as I learn, develop my skills, and complete my studies. I am not thinking about failure on this path, nor am I afraid. I am inspired by hope, curiosity, and purpose. How can I deny that I am having a "calling"? I don't have to do this, yet I am totally committed to my journey.

The so-called "failing moment" I shared appears to play an important part in my career journey. Discovering what didn't feel right and the lessons I learned in those experiences have offered me the growth and clarity I needed to recognize my true values and strengths and how to apply them to be of service to others. I am still traveling on my path, not sure exactly where it will take me, but I know I am supposed to be traveling in this direction. I look forward to seeing where I land and strive to positively impact the world around me.

I believe the inspiration that is propelling me down this new career path comes from my spiritual self. Perhaps, my "soft inner voice," my "gut feeling," and my "intuitive thoughts" are *indeed* a calling from God. This I am not sure of; however, I would like to believe so.

A man's heart plans his way, but the Lord directs his steps (Proverbs 16: 9 NKJV).

Though he fall, he shall not be utterly cast down; For the Lord upholds him with His hand (Psalms 37:24 NKJV).

Be strong and of good courage do not fear nor be afraid of them: for the Lord, your God, He is the One who goes with you. He will not leave you nor forsake you (Deuteronomy 31:6 NKJV).

For I consider that the sufferings of this present time are not worthy to be compared with the glory which shall be revealed in us (Romans 8:18 NKJV).

Closing Notes

By Dena Moscola

We all interpret God's messages in different ways. In *our* ways. The connecting link is that when we (or anyone) follow God, our lifestyle changes significantly and stays changed; our stress decreases, our hearts open more, and we commit our lives to learn more about and fulfilling God's purpose for us.

> I will give you a new heart and put a new spirit within you; I will take the heart of stone out of your flesh and give you a heart of flesh. I will put My Spirit within you and cause you to walk in My statutes, and you will keep My judgements and do them. Then you shall dwell in the land that I gave to your fathers; you shall be My people, and I will be your God. I will deliver you from all your uncleanness. I will call for the grain and multiply it and bring no famine upon you. And I will multiply the fruit of your trees and the increase of your fields, so that you need never again bear the reproach of famine among the nations (Ezekiel 36: 26 – 30 NKJV).

God is ready and waiting to have a relationship with you, despite your past, despite your thoughts, despite your age, despite it all.

And we have known and believed the love that God has for us. God is love, and he who abides in love abides in God, and God in him (1 John 4:16 NKJV).

For I know the thoughts that I think toward you, saith the Lord, thoughts of peace, and not of evil, to give you and expected end. Then shall ye call upon me, and ye shall go and pray unto me, and I will hearken unto you. And ye shall seek me, and find me, when ye shall search for me with all your heart. And I will be found of you, saith the Lord (Jeremiah 29:11–14).

You can count on God to love you each and every day. All you need to do is want him to!

Through the Lord's mercies we are not consumed, because His compassions fail not. They are new every morning: Great is Your faithfulness. "The Lord is my portion," says my soul, "Therefore I hope in Him!" The Lord is good to those who wait for Him, to the soul who seeks Him (Lamentations 3:22-25 NKJV).

'For the mountains shall depart and the hills be removed, but My kindness shall not depart from you, nor shall my covenant of peace be removed,' Says the Lord, who has mercy on you (Isaiah 54: 10 NKJV).

But You, O Lord, are a God full of compassion, and gracious, longsuffering and abundant in mercy and truth (Psalm 86:15 NKJV).

Therefore know that the Lord your God, He is God, the faithful God who keeps covenant and mercy for a thousand generations with those who love Him and keep His commandments (Deuteronomy 7:9 NKJV).

Meet Dena Moscola

With a passion to help others, Dena spent the first several years of her career in human services, helping adults with developmental disabilities in employment and residential settings. In 1997, after multiple management roles and numerous certifications, she founded Resolutions Coaching & Training, providing professional and personal development to leaders and their teams around the world. Topics she is most sought out for are leadership development, emotional intelligence, managing conflict and more. Dena has had 5 other books published.

Dena recently took a 2-year break from her business to start and manage a nonprofit organization serving those experiencing homelessness and addiction in a New Mexico city known as the Heroin Capital of the United States. At the Espanola Pathways Shelter, she led efforts to start their first homeless shelter, first transitional housing program and 1st SMART Recovery Program. During that time, she had the privilege of talking with many people about their walk with God. She and her team helped many understand that God wants us to know him and everyone is worthy of his love and guidance, despite their past. A few days after resigning from that role, Dena had a dream 3 nights in a row, inspiring her to write this book. She believes God gave her the topic, outline and title in those dreams so she immediately went to work. Her intention for this book is to help others build a stronger relationship with God, no matter where they are in their faith.

Dena Moscola runs her virtual business,
Resolutions Coaching and Training,
while enjoying God's gifts and
living in beautiful Northern New Mexico.
Dena@ResolutionsCTC.com
www.ResolutionsCoachingandTraining.com

www.ingramcontent.com/pod-product-compliance
Lightning Source LLC
Chambersburg PA
CBHW051006140626
46546CB00016B/948